A SHORT
HISTORY OF
SUFFOLK

A SHORT HISTORY OF SUFFOLK

Derek Wilson

B. T. Batsford Ltd, *London*

First published 1977
© Derek Wilson, 1977
ISBN 0 7134 0574 0

Filmset by Elliott Bros. & Yeoman Ltd.,
Liverpool L24 9JL and
printed in Great Britain by
J. W. Arrowsmith Ltd., Bristol
for the publishers B. T. Batsford Ltd.,
4 Fitzhardinge Street, London W1H 0AH

CONTENTS

ACKNOWLEDGEMENTS

The Author and Publishers would like to thank the following for permission to use illustrations from their collections:

Abbots Hall Museum of Anglian Rural Life, Stowmarket (27, 29, 31–33); Hallam Ashley (12, 19, 25); D. H. Blowers (9–11, 15, 18, 26); Department of the Environment (8); A. F. Kersting (14); Peta Hambling (30); Lowestoft Public Library (28); Radio Times Hulton Picture Library (1); Kenneth Scowen (13); Victoria and Albert Museum (20); Trustees of the British Museum (2–6); Jeffery W. Whitelaw (16, 24). 7, 21, 22 and 23 are from the Publisher's collection.

To Cherie:

On Her Birthday.

Aua 24th 1983.

Dad.

LIST OF
ILLUSTRATIONS

(between pages 80 & 81)

PREFACE

The big skies leave the East Anglians empty. The skies are
nothing. The horizons are too wide. There is nothing for a
man to measure himself by here. In Scotland you have the
hills, the mountains. They diminish a man. They make him
think . . . He knows they last and that he doesn't. There is
nothing like this in East Anglia. The water moves in Scotland
but in Suffolk it stands still – or as good as. Because they are
a flat-land creature there is a lack of imagination and excite-
ment in the Suffolk character.

Few outsiders would express themselves in such extreme terms
as that immigrant from Scotland, yet his words formulate many
of the common prejudices and misunderstandings about the
land and people of Suffolk. Dull, unimaginative, slow, secre-
tive, unfriendly – these are supposed to be the attributes of
Suffolk folk. The country they inhabit is an unknown land
– unknown because it does not lie on the way to anywhere
and because it has no grandiose or dramatic scenery to attract
visitors.

The truth, of course, is more complex, more subtle. Can a
landscape be dull which has inspired England's greatest landscape painters and some of her better poets? Can her people be
unimaginative when they have built such architectural glories

as the great churches of Lavenham, Long Melford and Stoke by Nayland? No fewer than 366 towns and villages of Suffolk are classified as being of considerable architectural and historic importance. Can a county that twice in our island's history has led the nation in economic development – in the great days of the medieval cloth trade and in the 1970s – be labelled a stagnant backwater?

The history of Suffolk, through good times and bad, is crammed with incident and dignified by the careers of great men and women. In setting down that history in outline my only sorrow is that I have had to omit so much: Thomas Clarkson, the man who did more than any other to abolish slavery; Elizabeth Garrett Anderson, England's first woman doctor; Robert Grosseteste, the great Bishop of Lincoln and Ecclesiastical reformer; Richard Hakluyt, pioneer English geographer – they were all Suffolk people yet, alas, there has simply not been room in the following pages to mention them. The long and tragic 'tithe war'; the intriguing case of the murder in the red barn; the development of Suffolk windmills – agonizing inner debates led to their reluctant exclusion also. For my brief has been to make clear the sweep of Suffolk history. If I have not drawn your attention to some of the more interesting trees, I hope that, at least, I have enabled you to see the wood clearly.

Derek Wilson

January, 1976

SUFFOLK

N

N O R

Santon
Brandon Downham

Lakenheath

Little Ouse

Elveden
Euston

Barnham
Coney
Weston Hopton
Red
Barningham

Mildenhall
Honington

Icklingham
Ampton Gt.
Livermere Walsha
le-Wille

Ingham
Ixworth

Hengrave

A45

Kentford
Gi

Moulton
BURY ST.
EDMUNDS A45

Woolpit H

Dalham
Stowup
Stowmarket

Bradfield
St Clare

NEWMARKET

Lidgate
Bradfield
Combust

Battisfor
Tye

Rede
Cockfield

Hartest
Thorpe
Morieux
Hitch

Little
Bradley
Boxted
Bildeste

Lavenham
Chelswor

Kedington
Cavendish

Clare
Long
Melford
Lindsey

Haverhill
Kerse

Stoke-by-
Clare
Groton

Stour
Boxford

Sudbury

Stoke-by-
Nayland
Polstea

Stra
Nayland
S

E S S E X
Bures

~ARTHUR BANKS~

CAMBRIDGESHIRE

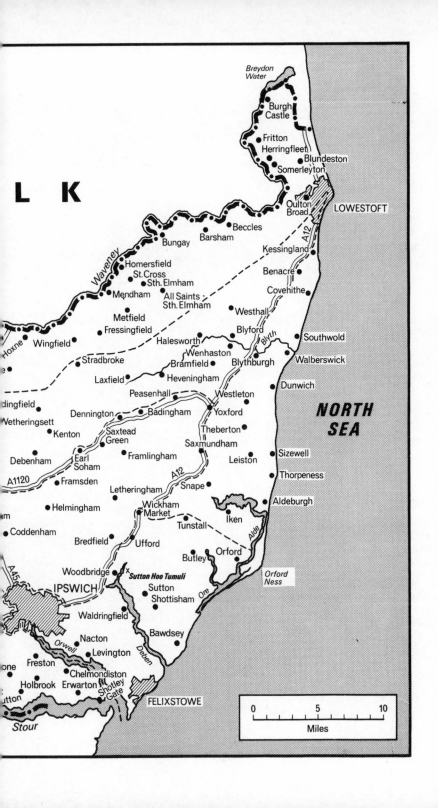

1. FOREST
AND FLINT

The search for oldest Suffolk begins at Staverton Thicks. Here ash, elder, hawthorn and briar plait themselves into an impenetrable jungle of undergrowth in the half-light granted them by centuries-old oak and elm. This is the last vestige of the primeval forest which once covered three-quarters of the county. Springing from the boulder clay deposited by the retreating ice-age glaciers this tangle of deciduous flora kept our hardy but unskilled ancestors at bay for thousands of years. Fifteen miles due west at Barking they claim to have the oldest tree in the county. The locals will tell you that Gospel Oak was already venerable when the first Christian missionaries preached beneath its shade to the devotees of Woden, Thunor and Frig. This arboreal patriarch has a few brothers and sisters which have survived to remind us of a very different past. Now they stand as isolated monuments in the rich open ploughland where scarcely a hedgerow is allowed to stand in the way of agricultural progress. Apart from these vanishing giants only place names such as Oakley and Occold, Eyke (Old Scandinavian for 'oak') and Elmsett remind us of the serried ranks of trunks and matted undergrowth which barred the way to the heart of Suffolk.

Yet, hundreds of thousands of the great trees are with us still. You would be hard put to it to find a single town or village without a sprinkling of oak-framed cottages, half-timbered farmhouses and the more impressive residences of the great wool barons. Nor is there a parish church which lacks rood screen, pulpit, roof timbering and pews of age-blackened Suffolk oak. This is where they have gone, those trees of old, or, at least, those which have not served to keep our ancestors warm or been felled to build the mighty walls of Drake and Hawkins, Jarvis and Nelson.

But that belongs to a later episode in a story that begins with the end of the last glacial epoch, about 10,000 years ago. It was then, when the forest was young, that man, following the ice sheet northwards, began the unbroken human occupation of what would one day be called Suffolk. It was then that the melting ice raised the level of the world's oceans and caused the North Sea to spill over into the Atlantic, thus severing Britain from the mainland and giving its eastery coastline the approximate shape it has today. East Anglia was then, as it has largely remained ever since, a closed land. It was on the way to nowhere and its habitable areas were protected by the forest and by the great fens to the west. There were only two ways into the region. Most settlers came by sea and found a hundred creeks and inlets giving access to a strip of marsh and heathland. From the rest of Britain the only entry lay along the ten-mile-wide chalk belt, running up from Berkshire to enter the county at Newmarket, pass through the sandy Breckland of Brandon and Thetford, then forge on to the Wash.

This was far from being the first period of human habitation, for Old Stone Age man was here 400,000 or 500,000 years ago. During the long interglacial epochs his descendants hunted bison, deer and wild pig with their crude flint weapons, while keeping well clear of wolf, lion and hairy mammoth. From the scanty remains of the human and animal inhabitants of Palaeolithic (Old Stone Age) East Anglia it is possible to piece together a fragmentary picture of what was obviously a very fluid population. Only when we reach the post-glacial or Mesolithic period does the picture become clearer. No longer do glaciers gouge gargantuan furrows through fossil-bearing

strata or bury others beneath fresh layers of soil. Henceforth the
buried warrior remained in his grave, the discarded bones of a
Stone Age feast stayed where they fell, the flint implements
stored by a hunter were not moved. They lie there still, below
the soil of Suffolk, in strata and locations which make the task of
interpretation a comparativey simple one for the archaeologist
who brings them to light.

East Anglian man of this period was still a hunter but a more
sophisticated one. He ranged the heathland, the river valleys
and the sparser woodland in small, highly mobile groups. He
and his companions lived in temporary camps and kept dogs to
help them track down wild pig, auroch, elk and deer. He snared
hare, badger, otter and fox for their fur and used bow and arrow
to bring down duck, goose and swan. For fishing expeditions he
took to the water in a dugout canoe from which he speared pike
with barbed harpoons of wood and bone or played the smaller
fish with rod and line. Sometimes he used nets with bark floats
or sank wicker traps to the beds of fast-flowing rivers. In summer a simple tent of stakes and skins was sufficient protection
for himself and his family, but the rains and snows of winter
demanded the building of huts of intertwined boughs layered
with turf.

It was not until about 4,500 years ago that the great agricultural revolution reached our shores. The techniques of pastoral
and arable farming had been learned ages before in the Middle
East and had given rise to the great civilisation of Egypt and
Mesopotamia. Slowly, by way of conquest and trade, the new
concept of man as the controlling centre of a malleable environment replaced the old conviction that the crowning glory of
creation was no more than a superior predator. The time of the
first farmers is called by archaeologists the Neolithic Age and it
lasted from *c*. 2500 B.C. to *c*. 1700 B.C. The newcomers landed on
the south and east coasts and made their way inland seeking
grass for their sheep and oxen and workable soil for their wheat
and barley. Their rate of progress and their distribution
depended largely on their relationships with the native
hunter-gatherers. There were, undoubtedy, many clashes pro-

voked by conflict of interest – an unsuccessful hunting party tempted by the browsing herds of the farmers; old stalking ground fenced off for pasture by the newcomers; competition for ownership of a fresh-water spring. But over the centuries there developed a degree of tolerance, co-operation, even intermarriage.

Neolithic man settled on the chalk and sandy heaths of the county's extremities. Evidence of his activities have been found around Ipswich and along the Gipping but more numerous and more interesting are the remains which have been unearthed along the Icknield Way.

England's oldest road was marked out by the unshod feet of Neolithic farmers and traders over 4,000 years ago. The route chose itself, for it followed the chalk ridge which offered the only corridor between the fen and the forest. From the edge of the Wash at Hunstanton it meandered southwards to the Breckland, swung away south-eastwards to cross Newmarket Heath, follow the Chiltern ridge to cross the Thames at Goring Gap and end at Marlborough Downs. Some of the men and women who used the Icknield Way were settlers and invaders, like the later Neolithic Beaker people whose journeys brought them from Belgium by way of the Norfolk coast and the ancient track to Avebury in Wiltshire, where their stone circle still reminds us of them. Most travellers, however, probably made comparatively short journeys along the Icknield Way coming, for instance, to buy high quality flint tools and weapons at Grimes Graves.

Grimes Graves, at Weeting, just over the Norfolk border from Brandon, is the site of England's oldest industry. Within 34 acres of heathland there are over 500 shafts and shallow depressions dug into the chalk by Neolithic man searching for flint. The growing population of farmers needed tools in abundance, for clearing trees and scrub, for turning the soil, for skinning animals and dressing hides, as well as for all the traditional uses of hunting and warfare. It was to meet this demand that generations of Breckland miners dug into the chalk to dislodge the flint.

The miners worked in small groups armed with stone axes and simple picks and crowbars fashioned from ox bones and the antlers of red deer. Their first excavations were shallow pits which yielded nodules of 'wall Stone', but experience taught them that the veins of 'floor stone' lying between 20 and 80 feet down were composed of a superior quality flint. So they dug wide shafts straight down through the crumbling chalk. When they reached the flint beds they followed them, digging as far as they dared through the soft rock with only their smoky oil lamps to illuminate the narrow, stuffy galleries. It was uncomfortable and dangerous work – as a skeleton found in a collapsed shaft at Whitlingham demonstrates. To ensure success and safety the earth deities had to be propitiated. In one of the pits at Grimes Graves the workmen built an altar and placed their antler picks on top in the hope that the earth goddess, represented in imagery by a pregnant woman, would bless their endeavours. The makeshift shrine was still intact when archaeologists discovered it over 4,000 years later.

Who were they, these Neolithic miners, pastoralists and farmers who lived in small semi-isolated communities on the edge of the forest and by the rivers of primeval Suffolk? The only names we have for them are the ones archaeologists have given them – Windmill Hill People, Rinyo-Clacton People, Bell Beaker People, Corded Ware People. We can distinguish different groups by their pottery, their burial customs and their tools. We know that there were many distinct groups. We can even deduce that there was some degree of intermarriage, or at least cultural mingling. But they have no identity, no individuality; they are mere shaded sections on the time chart of human progress.

The next broad band on that time chart is the Bronze Age. Bronze tools and weapons came late to Suffolk. Flint was here in abundance and the mines were worked for centuries but there was no copper and no tin. The first metal objects, therefore, had to come from abroad – from Germany and Ireland. They were brought by merchants trading the Icknield Way; by new settlers from across the sea; by itinerant herdsmen who interned their leaders' ashes within dramatic round barrows faced with gleaming chalk. Wandering smiths hawked their awls and axes, spearheads and daggers from village to village. They fashioned new tools from blunt and broken implements, but despite the obvious superiority of their wares they encountered considerable sales resistance among many Suffolk communities. The men of prehistoric Brandon and Mildenhall were still using stone tools in 500 B.C. and they were East Anglians who believed firmly in old and trusted methods.

But technological progress is always irresistible in the long term, if not in the short. The bronze smiths settled sites like Butley near Woodbridge, where people congregated regularly for markets or religious festivals, and where there was plenty of timber for the furnaces. They opened up new dimensions of life for their customers. The local people found that they could clear the land more easily with socketed axeheads, metal picks and sickles. They could make themselves wooden bowls, dishes and simple furniture by using the new saws, chisels and gouges. Warfare was transformed by their leaf-shaped slashing swords, battle axes, circular shields of sheet metal and peg-fastened spearheads. And cooking must have been revolutionized by the first cauldrons. So the Bronze Age culture spread, pushing back before it the limits of the forest and the stubborn Stone Age men who could not come to terms with change. By 500 B.C. life in Suffolk had changed out of all recognition. Settlements were larger and more permanent. Each homestead had its fenced pastures where flocks and herds were grazed for at least part of the year. The land, now turned by light ploughs, produced more abundant crops of barley and other cereals. Tamed ponies made Bronze Age folk more mobile than their predecessors. Trade became a more important feature of life now that surplus produce could be taken to market by cart. For the wealthier farmers and their wives there were decorated brooches, bracelets and cloak pins of bronze or – for a favoured élite – of gold. Clothing was more varied: no longer did people rely totally on skins; they spun, wove and dyed their own garments from wool and flax. When a loved one died they burned the body on a fun-

eral pyre and enclosed the ashes in a leather bag fastened with a
bronze pin, or in a pottery urn. This was buried unmarked in a
flat field or covered with a small cairn of stones. Only the more
important members of society were interred within large barrows like the 30 mounds on Brightwell and Martlesham
Heaths, east of Ipswich.

Bronze Age people were no strangers to violence. The pressures of an increase in population were building up in mainland
Europe. At about the time the Romans were founding their
Republic, bands of dispossessed people were fleeing across the
North Sea from the Low Countries. There was nothing new in
that; it had been happening for thousands of years. What *was*
new was that these latest invaders brought deadly new
weapons made of iron. They landed in the south-east and made
their way up the Stow, the Orwell, the Gipping and the Deben.
Having driven out the native settlers or found uninhabited
tracts of country, the newcomers built themselves round,
moated house-enclosures and settled peacefully to pick up the
pieces of their shattered lives.

Not so the next wave of Iron Age invaders. The Marnians (so
called because they originated at Marne in France) were war
lords – tall professional warriors with double-handed axes,
long swords and elaborate body armour – and they possessed a
terrifying weapon which revolutionized warfare – the chariot.
In the third century B.C. they came, landing in the Thames
estuary and the Wash and harrying their way inland, to settle
at last in the Breckland and adjacent areas. Theirs was a new
kind of society, one dominated by warrior chiefs like the tall fel-
low buried at Mildenhall with his sword, his axe, a gold torc
and his two most prized possessions – his chariot ponies. The
Marnians extended their rule over a large area of Norfolk, Suffolk and Cambridgeshire. With them the long dawn of prehis-
tory in Suffolk ends. For these warlike people were one of the
first in Britain to encounter the Romans and, therefore, one of
the first to enter the realm of written history with a name –
Iceni.

The Iceni, like their Iron Age contemporaries, were much

more sophisticated than their precursors. Military might gave them administrative organization. Differences of wealth and power created the need for tokens of rank – necklets, bangles, brooches and ear-rings of gold, elaborately decorated horse harness and mounts for swords and daggers fashioned with barbaric splendour from gold alloyed with silver or copper. Trade became both more organized and too sophisticated for simple barter to be an adequate medium for market transactions. At Santon Downham, Haverhill and Freckenham, hoards of gold and silver coins have been found bearing the names of tribal chiefs. Some came from the Low Countries but others were minted locally. All the archaeological evidence so far discovered, tells of a prosperous and well-ordered society.

The twin bases of this wealth were improved agriculture and slavery. Iron Age farmers used metal-shod ploughs, pulled by horses or oxen, which would break up the heaviest clay. Suffolk man was now equipped to reclaim as much of the forest as he wanted and to exploit it efficiently once it was reclaimed. He grew wheat, barley, oats and beans. He could store enough hay to see many of his cattle through the winter and if beef was ever scarce he could enjoy the flesh of sheep, goats, pigs and fowls as well as hunted animals. The peasant masses provided a source of cheap labour and ensured that efficient farmers had a trading surplus after harvest. This enabled them to buy the luxuries they craved – French wine, gold ornaments made by local and continental craftsmen, drinking vessels and enamelled horse trappings.

Much the same could be said of the people who dominated the south eastern part of the county. The Romans knew them as Trinovantes and, indeed, it was the Trinovantes who were instrumental in bringing the Romans to Britain. During the first century B.C. the peoples of East Anglia came under increasing pressure from the fierce Catuvellauni of the lower Thames valley. The Trinovantes lost battle after battle and were forced steadily northwards and eastwards, their herds stolen, their crops burned. Mandubracius, their king, knew that if his enemy, Cassivelaunus, was not stopped he would soon reach the ditches, ramparts and fences of the Trinovantes capital near modern Colchester. In tactical skill and sheer numbers the Catuvellauni were more than a match for the defenders and there was no-one he could turn to for help. Or was there? All the news coming across the sea from Europe had been of a formidable Roman general who had defeated, one by one, the great war lords of Gaul, including many of the Belgic cousins of the Catuvellauni. In 56 B.C. Mandubracius crossed the sea to place his people under the protection of Julius Caesar.

The first legions landed in Britain the following summer, but it was not until 55 B.C. that Caesar himself came to face the might of Cassivellaunus. The clash came somewhere in Kent and, for once, the great Roman's hopes of quick victory were frustrated. Confronted by skilful charioteers and horsemen who knew every inch of the ground, the legions were unable to compel their adversaries to a fixed, decisive battle. Now it was Caesar's turn to look for help. Employing the age-old colonial policy of 'divide and rule' he sent ambassadors to the Trinovantes and the Iceni offering permanent protection in return for support against the Catuvellauni. The support which Mandubracius gave was decisive. He led the Roman agents to Cassivellaunus' headquarters at Wheathampstead. The Romans marched rapidly northwards forcing their foes to choose between abandoning their capital or offering a pitched battle. They fought. They lost. They made terms. They undertook to leave the Iceni and Trinovantes in peace.

Any satisfaction Mandubracius' people may have felt at the outcome of events soon evaporated. Instead of establishing a permanent presence which would have compelled the Catuvellauni to behave themselves, the disciplined cohorts of Rome returned to their boats and sailed away from Britain – perhaps for ever. They did, in fact, come back after a hundred years, but not before the Catuvellauni had been able to take their revenge at leisure on their East Anglian neighbours. They made many raids into the territory of the Iceni and Trinovantes, but the most devastating came about A.D. 10 when Prince Cunobelinus (Shakespeare's Cymbeline) of the Catuvellauni broke away from his brother's rule, overran the Trinovantes and established an independent kingdom in north Essex and southern Suffolk with its headquarters at Camulodunum (Colchester). Having done this, he ousted his brother from the Catuvellauni throne and established himself as master of a united and enlarged kingdom.

Now it was the turn of the Iceni to be crushed by the relentless Catuvellauni advance. Cunobelinus led his people westwards to skirt the forest then turned north, driving his enemies out of Clare, Saffron Walden, Royston, Mildenhall and Thetford. Diminished and dispirited, the Iceni fell back into the woods and marshes of Norfolk, their total eclipse as an independent power looming over them. But their darkest hour proved to be the one before dawn. In A.D. 42 Cunobelinus died and in the following year the legions returned.

More than one Roman emperor had contemplated winning fresh glory for himself by taking up Julius Caesar's unfinished work in Britain, but it was the otherwise unremarkable Claudius who began the conquest proper of this island. His soldiers landed in Kent and soon made themselves masters of the more prosperous southern regions. Not that all the people acquiesced in this imperial take-over; the Catuvellauni confederation under their new leader Caractacus offered stiff resistance, but the ungloved iron hand of Rome pushed aside all opposition with ease. Brave and skilful as the British charioteers and infantry were, they were still using the uncoordinated tactics of earlier generations against masters of colonial warfare. Not only that, but they could not count on the support of all Britons; many tribes, among which were the Iceni and Trinovantes, placed themselves once more under Roman protection.

So rapid was Roman success that within weeks Claudius was able to come over, personally lead the assault on Camulodunum, and after a stay of sixteen days, depart again, to parade his captives through the streets of the eternal city. He was neither the first nor the last leader in history to take the glory for himself while leaving the hard work to subordinates.

The provincial governors and generals in Britain had to consolidate their grip on the south and east and then push forward to find and maintain a viable frontier. The agreements reached with the peoples north and south of the Thames were invaluable to the Romans as they pressed westwards and northwards to encounter the mounting opposition of the more hostile tribes. Camulodunum was nominated the capital of the province and rapidly grew – thanks to Trinovantes slave labour – into an impressive city. What a strange alien thing it must have seemed – a cold geometrical stone monument standing on open heathland, with massive walls and towers, huge portals, soaring arches, rigidly intersecting streets, theatre, public buildings and temples dedicated to foreign gods with unpronounceable names. The Trinovantes had exchanged one set of conquerors for another and their new masters were more demanding then ever the Catuvellauni had been. Soon they lost some of their best land: it was decided to make Camulodunum a colony for veteran soldiers and a large tract of country was confiscated to make agricultural holdings for the settlers. Smaller settlements and villas were built at Ipswich, Coddenham and numerous other sites.

The plight of the Iceni was less severe. The javelin-straight Roman roads did not yet intersect their territory. Separated from the Roman headquarters by the thick woodland of high Suffolk, they were able to maintain a degree of political independence. Their ruler, known to us as 'Saemu', from the abbreviated form of his name appearing on coins, was confirmed in office as a client king. For a few years the Iceni enjoyed all the benefits and few of the disadvantages of contact with a more advanced culture: they traded their surplus corn and meat to the Roman garrisons and villas; bought pots and metalwork of superior quality and new design; used the stable currency of the conquerors and copied many of their ideas.

The bond of peaceful co-operation was broken by Governor Ostorius Scapula who was determined on a showdown with Caractacus and his allies in the west and north. Since the major campaign he had in mind required every armed man he could

muster, his eastern base would be under-garrisoned. Therefore, to guard against trouble in his rear he sent posses of men
around the East Anglian tribes to confiscate, by force if necessary, all their armour and weapons. Iceni pride was outraged.
The warriors refused to give up the beautifully carved and
embossed swords and shields passed down from their ancestors
or to lose the bravely-decked chariots they prized so highly. To
a man they rose up against the presumptuous aliens. They were
swiftly crushed and their leader was replaced by the more
pliant Prasutagus, but the seeds of hatred had been sown.

The ripe fruit fell in A.D. 60. The widespread revolt of that
year, led by the legendary Boadicea (or Boudicca, to use the
style now favoured by scholars), was again provoked by the
insensitive and aggressive imperial power. Rome had decided
to end the semi-independence of the Iceni when Prasatugus
died. In anticipation of that event they clamped heavier and
heavier burdens on this proud and wealthy nation. The annual
tribute was steadily increased, grain and fatstock prices were
pegged at rates favourable to the Roman middlemen and an
army of credit-mongers battened on to the hard-pressed Iceni
nobility. The cautious Prasatugus tried to avert the disaster
threatening his kingdom. In his will he named the Emperor
Nero as heir to half his immense wealth hoping that his two
young daughters would be allowed to enjoy the remainder and
that a grateful emperor would permit Prasutagus' widow,
Boudicca, to succeed to the Iceni throne. The King's hopes
were shattered swiftly, suddenly and barbarically. As soon as
Prasatugus was dead a large force set out from Camulodunum
to seize his lands and possessions. They took over farms, threw
the nobles out of their homes, enslaved many able-bodied men
and women and behaved everywhere with a boorish contempt
for the 'barbarians'. When they reached the royal capital they
excelled themselves in senseless excesses. As the Roman
Tacitus admits 'nothing was exempted from their avarice,
nothing from their lust'. The palace was looted; Boudicca
flogged; and her daughters raped.

The outraged Iceni would stand no more. In the name of

vengeance and freedom they gathered together and placed themselves under the leadership of their tall, chestnut-haired Queen. From Boudicca's cold, flaming hatred they lit the torch of revolt, and Boudicca discovered in herself resources of courage and leadership which had lain dormant for years. With stealth, patience and cunning she laid plans for a rising which would not merely pay the Camulodunum garrison in its own coin, but would drive the Romans from the land. She organized and inspired not only the Iceni; by fenland causeways and forest paths the representatives of the Trinovantes, the Catuvellauni, the Dobuni, the Coritani and the Brigantes made their way to the Iceni capital. From there, news of the coming conflagration spread far and wide to the rulers of every tribe in occupied Britain, the messengers astonishingly slipping through the Roman net of spies and informers.

When the storm broke it struck a province which was totally unprepared. The Governor, Suetonius Paulinus, was 'pacifying' Wales with a large army. The depleted garrisons at Lincoln, Gloucester and Wroxeter had their own local situations to watch. Camulodunum had neither the defences nor the garrison to withstand a large-scale attack and if Camulodunum fell there was nothing to prevent tribesmen sweeping on to Verulamium (St Albans) and the virtually unguarded commercial centre of Londinium. Rumour and alarm reached the *colonia* at last and the veterans took thought for digging new ditches and throwing up earthworks. They were too late: Boudicca was mustering 100,000 warriors on the border of Suffolk and Norfolk.

In the Spring of A.D. 60 they moved southwards through the unsown fields. As they marched along the line of today's Norwich–Ipswich road they were joined by groups of Trinovantes. Boudicca's incredible magnetism kept her mongrel horde together and under firm discipline. Female leadership was about as unusual as inter-tribal co-operation among the Britons, yet the enormous army moved steadily forward, refraining from pillage of the smaller Roman settlements along the way. Not until they fell upon Camulodunum did the Britons give vent to their hatred. They swarmed over the walls, burned houses and shops, butchered men, women and children indiscriminately and forced the defenders back to the temple of Claudius where they made a last, desperate stand.

The efficient Roman military machine was soon set in motion. From Lincoln a detachment of the Ninth Legion set out under the leadership of Petilius Cerialis. They marched via Godmanchester and Cambridge towards the troubled area. Boudicca sent part of her host along the Stour valley to confront them, and the two armies met, probably somewhere on the Suffolk-Cambridge border. Cerialis' force of disciplined soldiery was cut to pieces, losing perhaps as many as 2,000 men. The legate himself fled back to Lincoln with the remnant of his cavalry, hotly pursued by the triumphant Britons.

The rest of Boudicca's story is of little immediate concern to us, acted out as it was in other parts of the country, but we must briefly relate the main events as a prelude to the terrible aftermath which came upon Suffolk and the surrounding areas. The British force, having tasted blood, rushed on to Verulamium and Londinium which suffered the same fate as the Roman capital. As victory followed victory, elation and self confidence took over Boudicca's host. Discipline became more difficult and the pursuance of clearly defined military objectives impossible. The initiative passed from the East Anglian queen to Suetinius. He had by now reached the disaffected area with the largest force he could muster. With the cold calculation of a trained strategist, he decided that his army was inadequate for an immediate encounter. This decision meant the abandonment of Londinium's 25,000 inhabitants to the fury of the barbarians and is clear proof of just how close Boudicca's revolt came to ousting the conquerors from Britain. The final battle came at last – we know not where – a battle which lasted all day and saw the overthrow of Boudicca's power-drunk host by the outnumbered, but highly disciplined legionaries. The Queen escaped to her own country and there died of disease or – if you prefer the more colourful version of legend – of remorse or poison, while her supporters were pursued through the land and cut down with merciless thoroughness.

Now it was the turn of Roman hatred and vengeance to be unleashed. Suetonius was determined to visit upon the Iceni and their friends a punishment so far out of proportion to the offence, that it would be remembered for centuries by Britons harbouring tentative thoughts of revolt. Southern and central East Anglia was systematically occupied. Temporary forts were thrown up at places like Coddenham and Pakenham and from these centres the angry centurions went on the rampage. Villages were burned, crops were destroyed and livestock slaughtered. The troops were given free rein to loot and pillage at will. At places as far apart as Santon, near Brandon, and Westhall, close to Halesworth, terrified landowners buried their treasure to keep it from the Romans – and never returned for it. In his determination to 'make the natives pay' Suetonius took no thought whatsoever for the future. It was the Procurator, Julius Alpinus Classicianus, who pointed out that the province had to be made to pay its way and that a sound administration had to be established. Neither would be possible if such highly productive areas as East Anglia were laid to waste and its people permanently ruined and alienated. Suetonius would not be convinced. A commission of enquiry had to be sent from Rome and only when this commission sided with Classicianus was the governor replaced and a more temperate rule established.

Whether it was the result of Suetonius' brutality or the leniency of his successors we cannot know, but Suffolk now enjoyed two centuries of quiet progress under the *Pax Romana*. The administration of the region had to be re-established from scratch after Suetonius' departure in A.D. 61. East Anglia was divided into two cantons more or less coinciding with the old Iceni and Trinovantes tribal areas. The northern canton was administered from *Venta Icenorum* (Caistor-by-Norwich); the other from Camulodunum or, possibly, from Coddenham. Tribal leaders were incorporated into the civil service system and the steady process of Romanization began. Metalled roads were built, the most important being the one linking Caistor to

Camulodunum. For the first time ever a major highway was cut across the centre of Suffolk. This was the Peddars Way which started, probably, at Camulodunum and passed through or near, Hitcham, Woolpit and Stowlangtoft to Thetford and thence to the Wash. Much of this road as, indeed, of the many minor roads which must have intersected the county 2,000 years ago, has long since passed under the plough. Looking at the strips which survive as grassed-over cart tracks, it is difficult to visualize the Peddars Way as a major military artery along which troops from Lincoln or Camulodunum could travel quickly to the heart of Iceni territory should the ancient fire of Boudicca once more stir her tribesmen's blood.

But most Romano-British remains in Suffolk bespeak the usages of peace and not of war. Villas inhabited by settlers and romanized British noblemen dotted the landscape. Towns such as Ipswich and Brettenham were established or grew out of earlier villages. Buildings were now timber-framed or even built of stone. New industries were developed. Iron ore was mined extensively while coincidence of clay and forest gave rise to important potteries at centres such as Wattisfield and West Stow (north of Bury St Edmunds). Peace and prosperity created a demand for a wider range of goods than had ever appeared before in East Anglia. Artifacts of pottery, bronze, iron, stone, marble and precious metals now reached Suffolk from all over Britain and the continent. Most imports probably reached Suffolk via London which rapidly overtook Camulodunum in size and became the capital of the province, but Ipswich and Camulodunum were thriving commercial centres and, early in the second century, Caister-by-Yarmouth was founded for trade with the Rhineland.

Yet, for all the evidence of Roman material civilization and contact with the wider world of the Empire, it is doubtful whether the influence of the foreigners cut very deep into the cultural soil of east Britain. The sons of noblemen might be sent off for education in Rome and return as members of a 'civilized' élite enjoying special privileges, but such a class formed a barrier between rulers and ruled rather than a vehicle of assimilation. Roman gods might be worshipped in the temples but so much religious syncretism had taken place that any visitor from Italy must have had difficulty in recognizing as his own the deities worshipped here. There were no major urban centres in Suffolk; Ipswich, Coddenham and Pakenham were no more than small market towns. Though the countryside was dotted with villas and large farms, few of these can be regarded as points of cultural diffusion, for most of them were probably run by managers on behalf of absentee landlords. The Romans were here for 400 years but little of their cultural heritage survived.

The ultimate challenge to Roman rule did not, however, come from within. It is significant that the most impressive surviving remains of the period testify to the decline rather than the might of Rome. In the extreme north-east of the county the massive walls of Burgh Castle gaze across Breydon Water into Norfolk. They are virtually all that remain in England of the 'forts of the Saxon shore', eleven bastions set up from the Wash to the Solent to guard our coast and our shipping from invaders and pirates. Their origin is always associated with the name of Carausius, as unmitigated a scoundrel as ever walked English turf. He was a skilful and shrewd Belgic pilot who rose rapidly in the service of Rome during the middle years of the third century – a time when the emperors needed every talented servant they could find to help withstand the barbarian tribes of northern Europe. About A.D. 286 the Emperor Maximilian appointed Carausius Count of the Saxon shore. This status gave Carausius command of the Classis Britannicus, the Roman Channel Fleet, and the coastal fortifications on both sides of the water. His main task was to stop Frankish and Saxon marauders raiding settlements. But Carausius had other plans; he decided to use his authority and the military resources at his command to enrich himself. Instead of challenging pirate vessels on their outward journey his ships waited until the vessels were making their sluggish homeward journey laden to the gunwales with booty. Only when he had possessed himself of the plate and the coin, the cattle, pottery and slaves did

Carausius do his duty and send pirates and pirate ships to the bottom.

It was not long before news of Carausius' activities reached Rome and an order went out for the admiral's arrest and punishment. Carausius countered boldly. He came to Britain, gained the backing of the legions stationed here and named himself *Imperator*. For six years Carausius was invincible. Not only did he command powerful land and sea forces, he also reinforced his position by making alliances with those very Saxons he was supposed to be guarding the Empire against. It may even be true, as some historians suggest, that Burgh Castle and its sister forts were built not to guard a Roman province from the barbarians but to guard Carausius from the forces of the legimate emperor.

Whatever the truth of the matter it is clear that when the shore forts were built the remoter parts of the Empire such as Britain were growing weaker as a result of pressure from without and corruption within. Carausius was, appropriately, stabbed in the back by one of his own subordinates, who then briefly assumed the purple. In A.D. 296 Constantius restored Britain to the Empire, but the times of peace, prosperity and progress were past. No major incursion or temporary conquest disturbed the pattern of life in East Anglia during the next century, but the economy gradually wound down as more and more troops were withdrawn and anxiety for the future mounted. Settlers left, entrusting their farms to tenants and bailiffs. Town populations declined. Worship at the temples languished, as though the gods, too, were going home. The outer skin of Roman civilization shredded rapidly away.

In A.D. 367 a co-ordinated three-pronged attack on the province by Saxons, Picts and Scots laid waste large areas. Roman forces were defeated by land and sea, and the Count of the Saxon shore was killed. No evidence has yet come to light to indicate a deep incursion of Suffolk at this time, but when Count Theodosius arrived from Rome to restore order, one of his first priorities was to strengthen the coastal defences by erecting a series of watch towers between the existing forts. The remains of one of these forts survive at Corton, near Lowestoft.

But little serious thought could be given to the permanent defence of Britain. More and more crack troops were withdrawn to fight battles nearer home. Their place was taken by barbarian mercenaries known as *foedarati*, cousins of those Saxon and Frankish warriors who were threatening the very existence of the Empire. They received grants of land in return for their military service, and settled alongside their Romano-British neighbours. They made their own encampments and townships, often beside Roman towns and forts. Slowly the population pattern changed; imperceptibly, Anglo-Saxon culture replaced Romano-British culture, softening the ground for the ploughshares of invasion. Many old families fled and others were forced off their farms by greedy Saxon neighbours. Land which had been under the plough for generations reverted to waste. Subsistence farmers scratched at soil which once had been scientifically farmed. Grass grew over the walls of deserted towns and overlaid stones worn smooth by centuries of tramping legionaries.

Yet from this time of desolation and decay comes the greatest monument to Romano-British civilization. Some time in the dark years at the beginning of the fifth century a wealthy farming family of Mildenhall fled hurriedly from their villa. Perhaps they hoped to return when the raiders, whoever they were, had gone. But they never did return and that is why their hastily buried treasures remained undisturbed for 1500 years. A Suffolk labourer, digging for victory during World War II, suddenly struck metal. The uninteresting lumps of dull, encrusted 'pewter' turned out to be 34 pieces of exquisite, highly ornamental silverware, mostly of Mediterranean origin. The Mildenhall Treasure is the finest hoard of Roman works of art ever found in Britain.

2 MEN OF FEAR
AND MEN OF
FAITH

'The Dark Ages' is a term rightly frowned on by historians. The implication that when the light of Roman civilization was extinguished Europe was plunged into four centuries of barbaric, heathen gloom can no longer be accepted. The Romans were conquerors. So were the Goths, the Vandals, the Angles, the Saxons and the Jutes. The Romans were technically more advanced. They had a written language and the 'barbarians' did not. And there any valid contrast ends. The newcomers had viable systems of commerce and agriculture. They had a vivid culture, expressed through the mouths of bards and poets and the hands of craftsmen in wood, bronze, iron, gold and stone. In one sense only can the period 400–800 be considered as a step backwards: it marked a return to prehistoric times. In Britain, at least, the new settlers left no written records of themselves and their activities. As with the pre-Roman British tribes, we rely upon archaeology, faintly illuminated by the Latin writings of a few monastic chroniclers, to tell the story of those four centuries. Fortunately Suffolk is very rich in sites of this period and, while much room remains for conjecture about the Anglo-Saxon kingdoms of East Anglia, there is a large corpus of established fact.

The Roman shore forts were finally abandoned in 407. At that time the inhabited parts of Suffolk were occupied by

British peasants and a landowning class comprising British and *foederati* elements. The two racial groups dwelt uneasily together but they had one common interest – to protect their land from seaborne invasion. It was now a case of every man for himself; centralized authority had collapsed and there was no possibility that the old Roman province could be ruled as one political unit. In Kent a local chieftain called Vortigern tried to rally support for the defence of the whole territory but his efforts only hastened the process of political disintegration. In order to fend off the incursions of the Picts and the Scots he invited more *feoderati* and rewarded them with land in East Anglia and around the Thames estuary. Inevitably, once the men from the north had been thrown back, Vortigern's allies turned on him and swarmed over eastern England carving out independent estates and kingdoms for themselves. Now the floodgates were opened and a succession of warlords crossed the North Sea in their long shallow-draught boats to probe the coast, rivers and inlets of East Anglia in search of land which was vacant or which could be made vacant.

Who were these Anglo-Saxons from whom the greater part of our present population is descended? They were fishermen-farmers from Schleswig Holstein, North Germany, the North Frisian Islands and, perhaps, from Denmark. Pottery finds suggest that we are here dealing with quite a large number of distinct communities who came severally and over a long period of years in their 70-foot-long, oar-propelled boats. This was no concerted invasion, but a piecemeal settlement similar to that of the Celts which had taken place over the millenia 'before the Roman came from Rye'. They rowed far up the rivers, first advancing from the Wash and penetrating the Breckland. Later raiders pushed up the Deben, the Gipping and the Orwell to establish settlements on the Sandlings.

The new culture established itself rapidly and completely. All Latin traces vanished. British landowners fled westwards or established a *modus vivendi* with the strangers. The peasantry found it easier simply to adopt the language and customs of their new masters. Old names were soon lost without trace and new ones appeared – *Gipeswic* ('the settlement by the estuary' – Ipswich), *Wudebrige* ('the wooden bridge' – Woodbridge), *Sudbyrig* ('the southern fort' – Sudbury), *Gyxeweorde* ('Gicsa's homestead' – Ixworth). 'Wic', 'Tun', 'weorde' – they are all words indicating small settlements, fortified homesteads where single families lived with their servants. The newcomers had no word for town since the concept of urban life and the complex social interrelationships it implied was alien to them. They lived in small self-sufficient units, in round houses of timber and thatch within stockades which provided shelter for man and beast. Hearth and home is very much an Anglo-Saxon idea. The communal fire was the centre of every homestead. The chiefs dwelt in more imposing timber halls where they feasted their warriors, discussed forthcoming campaigns and listened to songs of ancient valour.

Early in the sixth century a group of settlers arrived in the Sandlings who were different from their predecessors. They came from Sweden and their leader's name was Wehha. Whether they were simply more aggressive than other groups or whether overcrowding in the Ipswich region forced on them the role of conquerors we do not know. What we do know is that Wehha's family, the Wuffings, established the first Kingdom of East Anglia. From their base at Rendlesham they ranged along the coast and rivers forcing their will on all the settlements, demanding allegiance and the payment of tribute (an early example of the protection racket!). Within fifty years the Wuffings had brought most of East Anglia under their sway and the Kingdom reached its zenith during the reign of Raedwald (*c*. 599–625).

Was it Raedwald or a later seventh-century king who was commemorated with incredible splendour at Sutton Hoo? When, in 1939, archaeologists opened a long barrow near Woodbridge they unearthed not only a magnificent collection of Anglo-Saxon treasures of enormous historical significance; they also exposed a whole new series of problems. The Sutton Hoo 'burial' is, justifiably, the most famous of all British archaeological discoveries. Sometime in the early seventh cen-

tury (between *c*. 625 and *c*. 670 according to the experts) a
Wuffinga king died. His people took an old longboat, 86 feet
long, draggged it on rollers to the royal burial ground overlooking the Deben, and lowered it into a specially dug trench. Then
into a cabin, erected amidships, they carried all their beloved
leader's possessions – his axe, jewelled sword, knife and spears,
magnificent helmet or iron and bronze, shield, stone sceptre
tipped with a fine bronze stag, leather and linen parade dress
with gold buckles and other accoutrements, a purse decorated
with panels of gold and enamel, six-stringed harp, drinking
horns mounted in gilt, dishes and bowls of silver, bronze cauldrons and hanging bowls, wooden cups, combs, clothes, a large
hoard of coins, even his pillow stuffed with goose down. It is all
very reminiscent of the event described in the poem Beowulf
(which may well have been part of the standard repertoire of
seventh-century minstrels):

> There at the haven, stood a ring-prowed ship –
> The radiant and eager ship of the lord.
> They laid down the beloved lord,
> The giver of rings, in the lap of this ship,
> The lord by the mast. They brought from afar
> Many great treasures and costly trappings.
> I have never heard of a ship of this size so richly furnished
> With weapons of war, armour of battles,
> Swords and corslets. Many treasures lay
> Piled on his breast . . .

Only they weren't! The fabulous treasures were not piled on the
king's breast, for the one thing missing from this 'burial' is a
body, and therein lies the greatest mystery of Sutton Hoo. Were
the king's remains not available for burial; lost in a storm at sea,
perhaps? Or is there a more intriguing solution to the mystery?
Does the Sutton Hoo memorial represent a culture in transition, poised between paganism and Christianity? The existence
of two silver christening spoons in the ship suggests that the
king had received Christian baptism. The missionaries admit-
ted to his kingdom would have taught him that the soul had no

need of earthly treasures after death. But old beliefs and customs die hard and the king's people might well have equipped a long ship with all the necessities for a journey into the unknown. While obeying the new God of the monks there was no need to turn one's back on the old ancestral gods.

Christianity entered Suffolk during the reign of Raedwald. In 597 Augustine and his monks had begun the evangelization of Britain, early achieving a signal success in the baptism of King Aethelbert of Kent. England was by this time divided into seven Anglo-Saxon kingdoms (the Heptarchy) and Aethelbert was recognized as the senior ruler, or Bretwalda. He was thus Raedwald's overlord and when he ordered the East Anglian king to be baptized Raedwald complied. The 'conversion', however, did not go very deep and the queen's devotion to the old ways ensured that her husband would only regard the Christian God as a recruit to the company of Woden, Thunor and Frig. But the two religions were now locked in a combat which would prove fatal for one or the other. Raedwald's successor, Eorpwald, embraced Christianity only to be murdered by a pagan usurper, Ricbert. Within three years the rightful heir, Sigebert, had returned from exile in the lands of the Franks and regained the throne. The new king was an impressive and much loved figure. He had the warrior skills of the Wuffingas allied with a religious devotion and a love of books which earned him the name Sigebert the Learned. The Christian teachers and the schools he had encountered in exile had made a profound impression on him and when he returned home he set Christian missionaries to work converting and educating his people.

St Felix and St Fursey were the Castor and Pollux of the evangelization of East Anglia. Though united in their common purpose, the two missionaries were as unlike as real twins sometimes are. Felix, the sophisticated Burgundian brought up in Frankish schools, an habitué of royal courts, was appointed Bishop of East Anglia by Archbishop Honorius in about 631. He established his base at Dummoc, an unidentified spot on the coast, variously located by scholars at Dunwich and Walton

Castle. There he built a cathedral and a school, and then set out as a Christian strategist to win the scattered souls of his large diocese. For seventeen years he laboured steadily – 'a pious cultivator of the spiritual field', as Bede calls him.

Fursey was an Irish monk, aflame with Celtic zeal and mysticism. After receiving a vision of heaven and hell as a young man he turned his back on home and comfort to become a wandering preacher. When he reached East Anglia, news of his holy life and heart-piercing eloquence soon came to Sigebert's ears. He entreated the saint to stay, and gave him the useless site of Burgh Castle as a base for his missionary work. There, on that desolate coast, Fursey built his monastery using the stone of the ruined fort and timber from the forest edge. There his little community imposed upon themselves the full rigours of the strictest ascetic discipline. Food, clothing and sleep alike were frugal so as not to distract the monks from worship, meditation and devoted service. For ten years Fursey preached his way round East Anglia, winning hundreds with his exaltation of the love of God and his vivid descriptions of eternal bliss and damnation. Then he was on the move again and died, at last, in the land of the Franks.

Fursey had a momentous influence on King Sigebert. Impressed by the teaching of the monks, the King resigned his pomp and power in order to take the cowl. These were difficult times for rulers to follow their own fancies, however pious. The conflict between the kingdoms of the Heptarchy had evolved into a struggle between the great states of Mercia, Wessex and Northumbria, with the other kingdoms being little more than pawns in the game. At the time when Sigebert vacated his throne, Mercia, under its mighty pagan king, Penda, was in the ascendant and in the 630s his forces were pressing hard on the East Anglian border. You can still see traces of the earthworks thrown up by the combined South Folk and North Folk. There were four lines of defence traversing the limestone ridge and obviously devised to fill the gaps between natural obstacles such as fen, forest and high ground through which the invaders had to come. The traveller between Royston and Newmarket can see them still: the Brand Ditch runs between Melbourne and Heydon; the Pampisford Ditch stretches for two miles from Pampisford towards Hadstock; the Flean Dyke connects Balsham and Fen Ditton ('Fen Ditch-end'). The most impressive, and obviously most important of all, was the Devil's Dyke. It begins at Reach on the fen and runs for seven miles, crossing Newmarket Heath just west of the town to the higher, forested ground at Woodditton ('Wood-by-the-Ditch'). Even after the weathering of centuries it is a formidable barrier; the rampart stands over six metres high, but the climb from the foot of the wide ditch before it is ten metres. Any attacker successfully scaling this formidable wall of chalk unscathed by the rain of spears and boulders would find himself standing, breathless, on the four-metre-wide rim with ferocious defenders before him and a long drop behind.

The first major crisis came in 636. The Mercians invaded in force and the East Anglians mustered to meet the challenge. But they had no confidence in their new king, Ecgric, and some of them went to Beodricsworth (modern Bury St Edmunds) Abbey to plead with Sigebert to lead them against the foe. But Sigebert the Learned refused to forsake the holy life and eventually his frenzied countrymen forced him to leave the cloister in his habit, hoping that his very presence on the field of battle would inspire the East Anglians. Hurriedly they marched eastwards and met the Mercians at some unknown point on the Icknield Way. Sigebert did not desert his people but he refused to forsake his vows. He would take neither armour nor weapon and went into battle equipped only with a stout stick. The battle was soon over. Both Sigebert and Egric were among the slain and their people were routed.

Penda now placed on the throne Anna, a nephew of the great Raedwald, to rule East Anglia as a Mercian vassal. Anna, like his predecessor, was renowned more for his piety than his warlike qualities. He sired four daughters each of whom excelled him in devotion by either taking up the religious life or founding monasteries and nunneries. Anna spent much of his time at his manor at Exning and may have made it his capital. The site near Newmarket had many advantages. It lay near the centre of the Devil's Dyke defence line. It was a good rallying point for military contingents of the North Folk and South Folk. It was not far from the important religious centre established by St Felix at Soham.

The strategic nature of Exning was put to the test in 654 when Anna fell foul of his overlord. Penda's Mercian hordes once more marched along the Icknield Way and Anna prepared to defend the Devil's Dyke. Recent archaeological activity has uncovered a large burial ground of the period and many of the skeletons bear the marks of violence. How long did the defenders withstand the siege before a vital breach was made in their line? Or is the *Anglo Saxon Chronicle* correct in stating that treachery played a part in Anna's downfall? We shall never know. All we can say is that the Devil's Dyke was crossed and that the Mercians pursued their fleeing opponents back to the capital and beyond. For more than 50 miles the chase went on through the field and forest, over heathland and ill-defined tracks until Anna and his remnant were brought to battle near Blythborough. There, according to the ancient chronicler, Henry of Huntingdon, Penda fell upon the East Anglians 'like a wolf on timorous sheep, so that Anna and his host were devoured by his sword in a moment, and scarcely a man of them survived'.

After the disaster of 654 little is recorded about East Anglia in the chronicles, a silence which we can interpret either favourably or otherwise. On the other hand, it would appear that the last generations of the Wuffinga dynasty, as happens to all families which have had a long tenure of power, produced no men of stature to compare with the founders of the house. The last Wuffing king died almost a hundred years after Anna and that century produced few events which the monastic scribes thought worthy of record. On the other hand the people of East Anglia seem to have been left in peace. Though owing allegiance to the kings of Mercia, they were far enough away from the main arena of political and military conflict to be left much to their own devices. Trade with the continent continued and in the eighth century the minting of silver coins called *sceat-tas* began in East Anglia. These coins have been found over a wide area of Frisia and north Germany while imported items of bronze, iron and pottery have been excavated from East Anglian sites. Ipswich was almost certainly the leading port and industrial centre of the region. Kilns discovered there once produced large quantities of pottery which were diffused over a wide area of England and northern Europe. Dunwich, too, was a thriving port and could afford to pay the king an annual rent of 60,000 herrings. Clearly economic depression did not follow on social decline.

It was during this period that Norfolk and Suffolk began to emerge as distinct entities. There had always been differences between the peoples north and south of the Waveney and these differences asserted themselves more as the power of the Wuffings declined. This was recognized in the spiritual realm about 673 when Archbishop Theodore divided the East Anglian diocese. A new ecclesiastical seat was established at North Elmham while Suffolk's church continued to be administered from Dummoc.

Christianity was now part of the fabric of English life. Preachers were sent out from Dummoc on regular tours. The monks of Burgh Castle, Soham and Beodericsworth ministered to the souls in their immediate localities and they wandered the hamlets of Suffolk to preach the Gospel and administer the sacraments. Nor were these the only religious houses of early date in Suffolk. In the year that King Anna died, Botolph built a monastery on the Alde estuary at Iken, and not far from the present county boundary a Suffolk princess established a house of prayer destined to become famous and to last over 1300 years. Aetheldreda was a daughter of King Anna and at an early age she fell under the spell of holy Felix and his monks. Her only ambition was to lead a life devoted to contemplation and prayer. But in Saxon society princesses were even less free than other women to follow their own inclinations. Aetheldreda was married off – first to a fenland earldorman and, after his death, to Prince Egfrid of Northumbria. If legend is to be believed, she survived both these 'unions' with her virginity intact, an achievement regarded as symptomatic of a very holy life in the quaint theology of those days. After twelve years, a frustrated and infuriated Egfrid gave his wife her freedom. Aetheldreda went straight to the lonely Isle of Ely and there, in that spot isolated from the world by river, marsh and fen, she founded a double monastery for monks and nuns and presided over it as the first abbess.

We would be wrong if we thought of these early Saxon Christians as worshipping in impressive stone churches and minsters bearing any similarity to those built by a later age. The first Suffolk churches were for the most part very simple affairs of wood and thatch. Stone is not a natural building material here, and only where earlier edifices existed in the form of disused fortifications or pagan shrines was the more permanent material used. As we can see from the story of Aetheldreda, religious impulses did not always come from the ecclesiastical hierarchy. It was largely lay piety which established the beginnings of the parochial system. Saxon landlords often asked the bishop to provide them with priests. They would build their own little churches so that they, their households and their peasants could be ministered unto. Sometimes it was the simple folk themselves who raised the first churches and then more for reasons of personal comfort than devotion. Services were originally held in the open and the only permanent feature was the altar, often converted from an old pagan shrine. Regular attendance in virtually all weathers was expected by the church and often commanded by the lord. It did not take long for the villagers to decide to build themselves a barn-like structure before the altar to protect themselves from the elements while they attended to the holy mysteries. Thus the first naves were built and thus, too, the custom evolved of regarding the nave of the church as the responsibility of the parish while the maintenance of the sanctuary was the priest's concern.

With the backing of the king and the great lords Christianity passed rapidly from the age of missionary zeal to the age of the established religion. The upkeep of churches and clergy was met by grants of land and by special levies approved by royal writ. 'Plough-alms' was a penny for every plough team and was payable fifteen days before Easter. Church-scot, the principal ecclesiastical levy, fell due at Martinmas (11 November) and fortunate, indeed, was that landholder who went 'scot-free'. Tithes of produce and stock were originally non-obligatory donations for the relief of the poor and needy but before many decades had passed they, too, had become sanctified by law. Perhaps most unpleasant of all ecclesiastical taxes was 'soul scot', the burial fee which, we are told was 'best paid at the open grave'. Yet it was all part of a pattern. The eighth century was not an age free from turmoil yet such local and national conflicts as did occur took place against a background of stable and established relationships. Priest and layman, thane and churl, warrior and monk – everyman knew his place in society, knew what his God and his king required of him. Was it a decadent society, a society going soft, as Bede suggested was happening further north?

As peace and prosperity prevail in these days, many of the Northumbrians, both noble and simple, together with their children, have laid aside their weapons, preferring to receive the tonsure and take monastic vows rather than study the arts of war. What the results of this will be will be seen in the next generation.

Whether or not East Anglia's military preparedness left something to be desired, it is certain that the region could not have withstood the next stampede of violent invaders. Out of the north they came – more warriors from the fringes of the Baltic. Norsemen, Vikings, Danes – they have many names but one overriding characteristic in the eyes of contemporaries: 'We and our forefathers have lived here for 350 years and never have terrors like these appeared in Britain; it was not thought possible that such havoc should be made.'

They came first to raid and plunder in the tall-prowed sailing ships that had carried the sea rovers to the Mediterranean and the coasts of America. For fifty years their sporadic visits devastated small coastal areas. During that half century the Viking war lords probed the strengths and weaknesses of the Anglo-Saxon kingdoms. Then, in 865, they came to stay.

Ivan the Boneless and his brother Halfdene landed on the Suffolk coast at the head of the 'great heathen army'. The terrified Anglo-Saxons fell back before the invaders. Those who had not seen the Vikings before had heard appalling stories of their barbarism. King Edmund sought peace and by the terms of the treaty the Danes were allowed to winter in Suffolk and assured of horses to carry their baggage. Edmund's speedy capitulation may have lacked valour but it saved his people much suffering. For several months the Norsemen consolidated their position and prepared for the next campaigning season. In the Spring Edmund's people watched with sighs of relief as their unwanted guests departed westwards to attack Northumbria and Mercia.

But the great army returned in 869 laden with spoil, flushed with triumph and heedless of former treaties. They wintered at Thetford and used it as a base from which to ravage the farms and, especially, the monasteries of a wide area of East Anglia. Edmund could not honourably allow this Viking rampage to go unchecked. He came forth to do battle with the heathen invaders and thus an insignificant king became a martyr, a saint and a legend.

A people in adversity needs its heroes; if live ones are lacking they may make do with dead ones. It was Edmund's fortune to achieve greater fame in death than in life. Pious legends, well sprinkled with miracles and signs, are our only source of information for that campaign of 869. A great battle was fought near Thetford. It lasted, according to Roger of Wendover, from dawn till dusk, 'till the stricken field was red with blood of the countless numbers who perished'. Edmund, it would seem, won the day but not long afterwards we find him and his bodyguard besieged in the Saxon fort at Framlingham which once topped the mound where the castle now stands. He made good his escape and fled northwards. Thereafter fact becomes submerged beneath a sea of romantic anecdote. There is even confusion over places. Some accounts portray Edmund as a deliberate martyr, surrendering himself to save his people further suffering. Others recount how, on the contrary, the king escaped his enemies by cunning. The story is an amusing one and worth repeating. Having left his refuge, Edmund encountered a party of Danes who asked if he knew where the King was. 'He was in the fort before I left,' replied Edmund, and went on his way unmolested. But before very long he was caught, tortured and executed. Historians seem to be agreed that the site of Edmund's martyrdom (called 'Haegelisdun' in the chronicles) was Hellesdon near Norwich. They will never convince the people of Hoxne who for over a thousand years have claimed their village as the scene of the saint-king's last days. The story they tell is that Edmund was hiding beneath a bridge when a bridal party happened to cross the stream. Looking down the bride noticed a golden gleam in the water – the reflection of the King's golden spurs. She gave the game away and Edmund was taken. Ever since that day the stream has been called the Goldbrook and wedding parties have avoided the bridge lest the saint should prove to have a long memory.

When we come to consider the details of Edmund's death we are on firmer ground. The King's standard bearer was with his master to the end and related the details to Bishop Dunstan, on whose trustworthy evidence they were incorporated in the tenth-century *Passion of St Edmund.* According to this document, King Edmund 'was brought to a tree in the neighbourhood, tied to it, and for a long while tortured with terrible lashes. But his constancy was unbroken, while without ceasing he called upon Christ with a broken voice.' This offended the pagan sensibilities of the Danes who further punished their bleeding victim by shooting arrows at him. His captors demanded that Edmund should renounce his Christian faith. 'Know you not that I have power to kill you?' the infuriated Danish leader demanded. 'Know you not that I know how to die?' came the weak but firm reply.

At last they cut Edmund's head off. From that point popular legend takes over completely: the severed head was hidden, but it called out to the King's servants who discovered it being guarded by a wolf; the body was buried and a small chapel erected over it wherein miracles began, almost immediately, to be performed; when the body was removed to Beodericsworth Abbey early in the tenth century the head and body had perfectly reunited themselves and neither showed any signs of decomposition. Edmund became a folk hero for the whole oppressed English people; churches were dedicated to him and King Alfred issued memorial coins bearing his image.

The Edmund stories reveal clearly the barbarism and ferocity which accompanied the Danish invasion – a savagery made worse by the clash of two opposing cultures. The two decades after 865 were terrible years for the Christian English of eastern England. Churches and monasteries were razed to the ground; holy books burned and torn; wayside altars broken; monks, nuns and priest became fugitives; the people either abandoned their faith or met in secret to celebrate the holy mysteries.

But in 878 the Danish host, now led by Guthrum, came face to face with the armies of Alfred of Wessex, and Englishmen realized that the Danes were not an irresistible force. Slowly the tide of battle turned: at first, a truce (880) by which the greater part of eastern and northern England was recognized as Viking land, the Danelaw; then, a steady offensive under Alfred and his son, Edward, which, by 920, brought all England back under one rule for the first time since the departure of the Romans.

During this period the Danes became settlers rather than raiders. Guthrum rewarded his followers with land, instead of booty, and the newcomers settled down beside the Anglo-Saxons to form a common community. Guthrum ruled from Hadleigh and kept for himself a territory which included most of Suffolk. Throughout the Danelaw the two cultures merged. The Danish contribution to the resulting way of life was stronger in some areas than in others. In Suffolk it seems to have been minimal. The Danes settled almost exclusively in areas bordering the coast and rivers. Throughout the entire county there are only about 50 place names which derive from

Old Norse (the language of the settlers) and many of those are in the north-east corner of the county (Norfolk, by comparison, has almost 200 town and village names of Scandinavian origin), such as Lowestoft, Ashby and Ilketshall. As part of the 878 treaty Guthrum had agreed to receive Christian baptism so that even in those areas under new Danish landlords the faith of Christ was, at least, tolerated.

Peace returned. There was little fighting on Suffolk soil for a hundred years, though the year 884 witnessed the first major English naval victory, fought in the Stour estuary. This was when Alfred's new fleet pursued homeward a Danish party of seaborne raiders. Where the Stour and Orwell meet together to pour into the North Sea he caught up with them. During the battle which followed he captured sixteen Viking long-ships and slaughtered their crews while Guthrum's men watched helplessly from the headland still known as Bloody Point. In 918, when the final confrontation between the two kingdoms began, Suffolk, Essex and Norfolk surrendered to Edward without a battle.

With peace came prosperity and the chance to develop the economic potential of the county. Now that Suffolk was part of a unified kingdom it was ruled no longer by hereditary East Anglian kings but by viceroys or *earldormen*. They were responsible for collecting taxes and raising the local militia – the *fyrd* – when the king needed it. Under the earldormen a tolerably efficient system of local government and justice existed. Whether the system was a recent development or an ancient one evidenced for the first time by extant documents it is difficult to say. The shire was divided into administrative units called 'hundreds' each with its own regular court. Each hundred consisted of approximately 100 'carucates'. The carucate was the equivalent of that unit of land called the 'hide' in other parts of the country. It was necessarily vague, as were all measurements at that time, but was defined as that amount of land which could be cultivated with one plough in the course of the year.

The carucate (perhaps 100–120 acres) was enough land to

50

keep a self-sufficient family. The number of such families increased rapidly in the late Anglo-Saxon period and the forest diminished in direct proportion to this rise. By the time of the Domesday Survey (1086) the population was 20,491, which made Suffolk the most densely populated county in England with the possible exception of Middlesex. Rich soil, the influx of settlers and the long period of peace go most of the way towards explaining this dramatic development. Suffolk now entered on a period of prosperity which was to continue, with a few fluctuations, for 600 years.

Another tradition established in the pre-Norman age was the fierce independence of Suffolk folk. This was a shire of free farmers and small-holders. According to the Domesday record there were 7,460 freemen in Suffolk and only 900 serfs. The proportion of independent landholders to peasants was quite different in Norfolk and Suffolk from that in any other shire. Although the average freeman could boast only a little land – usually much less than a curucate – he could call himself his own man, something which has always meant a great deal to East Anglians. The land holdings were concentrated into compact blocks edged by markers or, sometimes, hedges. On them the farmers drove their ploughs pulled by dun oxen, and pastured their sheep, pigs and cattle. They might also have grazing rights on nearby heath and woodland. Every autumn they slaughtered most of their beasts and preserved the meat with salt from the saltpans on the Wash or the Stour estuary. Fowls, river fish and sea fish supplemented their diet. Wool hides from their own flocks and herds clothed them. Most of them achieved self-sufficiency and were left with a surplus for market.

Towns grew in this period. Their development was a natural process but was encouraged by central government which needed focal points where administrative business could be carried out and markets properly supervised. Ipswich, Dunwich, Bury St Edmunds, Sudbury and, just over the border, Thetford were the first centres which could be dignified with the name of town. Sudbury, whose importance was basically military, was the smallest, with a population of about 500. The ports of Dunwich and Ipswich could boast 3,000 and 1,300 respectively. Bury, with its revived monastic life, had about 3,000 inhabitants. Thetford, too, was an important monastic centre long before the transference of the episcopal seat there from Elmham at the end of the eleventh century and it had a population of about 5,000 (which is much the same figure as the present population). All of these with the exception of Dunwich were considered to be of sufficient importance for royal mints to be established in them.

The term *seelig* (holy) Suffolk is a very old one and there certainly seems to be some justification for it. On the eve of the Norman conquest there were something in the order of 400–500 churches in the county.* That is one for every fifty people, a statistic which dwarfs the figures for other shires. Can we explain this apparent piety? The comparatively thin Danish settlement may be one answer. The zealous activities of the monks and secular clergy is undoubtedly another. Yet there are another two further reasons which seem to me to be more compelling.

The church in Suffolk was a persecuted church. The ravages of the ninth century left it leaderless and put a permanent end to the bishopric of Dunwich. Even after the settlement of 878 the Christian faithful cannot have felt secure for many years and the East Anglian diocese was not recreated until 956. Although the Anglo-Saxon and Danish populations slowly cohered into a predominantly Christian community, their troubles were far from over. In 981 fresh Viking raids began. In 991, ninety-three boatloads of Norsemen landed on Suffolk soil. They burned Ipswich to the ground, then marched to Maldon in Essex where they met the English forces in the most momentous battle of the Anglo-Saxon period. In 1004 the invaders were back again and this time it was the turn of Thetford to be ruthlessly destroyed. However, before they could ravage further they were confronted by

---

*It is not possible to be accurate; this figure is derived from possible references to ecclesiastical buildings in the Domesday Book but the Norman surveyors were only interested in assessing people and land. There could have been many more churches.

Earldorman Ulfcytel and the East Anglian *fyrd*. After a bloody battle the Danes withdrew.

They were back again six years later for the final encounter. Thorkell the Tall landed at Ipswich and marched across Suffolk to meet Ulfcytel's force at Ringmere Heath near Thetford. The English stood little chance against Thorkell's superbly disciplined army. Some of them broke ranks almost immediately but the men of Cambridgeshire sold their lives dearly and the dead of both sides lay thick on the ground ere the battle was done. During the following months Suffolk and the surrounding lands were totally devastated. That is no exaggeration – crops, herds and flocks were so ravaged that not even the invaders could find food. They moved into Essex pursued by Ulfcytel. At Ashingdown hill the last battle was fought. The English were defeated and Ulfcytel was among the slain. East Anglia was once more under Danish domination and was mercilessly harried by the followers of King Swein Forkbeard. In 1016 the whole of England fell under the sway of his successor, Cnut (Canute), and was annexed to the Danish kingdom. Thus for a second time in 150 years the Christian culture in East Anglia came under determined pagan attack. Those weak in the faith quickly submitted but others shed their blood as martyrs and in so doing fed the tender plant of East Anglian Christianity.

The other reason for the strength of religion in Suffolk was the presence at Beodricsworth of England's premier shrine. The remains of St Edmund were moved to the abbey about 902 as a resting place more fitting for such holy relics. There they remained in a specially built shrine for many years and thousands of devout pilgrims came to pray and make offerings at the tomb of the national martyr-hero. The community prospered and soon owned a great deal of land around the town. It was therefore prudence as well as piety which caused them to send their holy asset away to London during Swein Forkbeard's devastation of East Anglia. The cult of the saint had by now taken firm hold of the minds of Englishmen, so much so that when the Danish king died suddenly it was confidently affirmed that Edmund had struck him down.

Cnut was a wise king who knew that if he wished the English to settle in peace under his rule he must respect their feelings. One of the ways in which he demonstrated a new, loving regard for his subjects was in the lavish generosity he bestowed upon the shrine of St Edmund. The saint's remains had been restored to the town which was now known as St Edmund's *Burgh* and the King now contributed liberally to a new church. More than that, he founded a new community of Benedictine monks to guard the shrine. In 1020 Uvius became the first Abbot of St Edmundsbury and in 1032 the new church was consecrated. Cnut himself came and made demonstrative reparation for the sins of his father. Not content with lavishing money and lands on the abbey and making it the richest in England, he offered his own crown on the altar and received it back in token that his rule had the blessing and support of the great saint. Edward the Confessor also felt a great reverence for the abbey. He exempted it from royal taxes and gave it jurisdiction over eight and a half hundreds – virtually the whole of western Suffolk. Where the king led, nobles, and other landowners followed. By the time of the Domesday survey the Abbey of St Edmund owned extensive estates in six counties. For a further four and a half centuries the abbey was to play a dominant – and not always fortunate – role in the life of the county.

3. CASTLES
AND CLOTH

William the Conqueror's followers, the last invaders of England, thought it necessary to impress the natives with their might. Throughout the land they erected castles, fitting monuments to their mastery. They were simple affairs at first – earth mounds (mottes), surrounded by ditches and surmounted by fenced enclosures (baileys). Within their wooden towers inside the baileys the foreign landlords felt secure from the Saxon peasantry. From these strongholds they sailed forth to fight for – and sometimes against – their king and to wage their own private battles against each other. In Suffolk the newcomers had little trouble with the people; the freemen and peasants of the county resigned themselves without a struggle to the exchange of a Danish conqueror for a Norman one. King William parcelled out his new domain to tenants-in-chief who, in turn, sub-let to others in return for payments in service or kind. Every substantial landholder built his own defensive stronghold. The men of Suffolk knew that it was futile to rise against the Normans; they knew how strong the new castles were – they had, after all, built them themselves under the watchful eyes of Norman overseers.

The first Norman castles have disappeared, most of them victims of urban or agricultural development. But some did not vanish; they changed. As generation succeeded generation the castles grew and altered to meet new demands and changed situations. Take Clare, for example. William I gave Richard FitzGilbert control of 170 manors in Essex and Suffolk, and FitzGilbert built his castle at Clare in the angle formed by the junction of the Stour and the Chilton. He used the massive 100-foot high motte of a Saxon earthwork and surmounted it by two baileys, each fenced and moated. Another moat and curtain wall encircled the base of the motte. It was a strong, defensive position but it did not satisfy twelfth-century owners who replaced the wooden tower with a stone keep and reinforced the curtain wall with four towers – Auditorstower, Constablestower, Maidenstower and Oxfordstower. The wall was pierced by elaborate gateways – Crowshouse, Redgate and Derngate. By the late thirteenth century the need was more for a prestige residence than a fortress. The keep spawned a variety of domestic offices and other buildings – stables, malthouse, servants' quarters, storehouses, kitchens and a chapel. Gardens, pools and a vineyard were laid out and in the fourteenth century accommodation was built in the outer bailey for hunting dogs and personnel, for the owners (now the de Burghs) and their guests were enthusiasts of the chase.

The owners of Clare castle were not central characters in the history of Suffolk. The Bigods of Framlingham and Bungay were. In 1066 King William appointed Ralph de Guader, an East Anglian nobleman of Breton origins, as earl of Norfolk and Suffolk. But Ralph was involved in an abortive rebellion nine years later and it was then that Bigods entered the history of our county. The King took the opportunity to reward a poor knight, Roger Bigod, for his loyalty to the crown by granting him the bulk of de Guader's confiscated estates (117 manors in Suffolk as well as other lands in the adjoining counties) and appointing him the royal steward in East Anglia. Had William been a prophet he would have bestowed his favour elsewhere. Roger was succeeded by his eldest son, William, but in 1120 disaster struck. That was the year of the *White Ship*. Henry I's only son, Prince William, set sail from Harfleur with 300 companions, the flower of English chivalry. The *White Ship* found-

ered and of all the company only a Norman butcher was left to
carry the tidings to Winchester.

> By none but me can the tale be told,
> The butcher of Rouen, poor Berold.
> (Lands are swayed by a King on a throne)
> 'Twas a royal train put forth to sea,
> Yet the tale can be told by none but me.
> (The sea hath no King but God alone.)

William Bigod, High Steward of England, was among the gay,
doomed company of the *White Ship*.

He was succeeded by his brother, Hugh, of whom it has been
said, 'he appears to have surpassed his fellows in acts of deser-
tion and treachery, and to have been never more in his element
than when in rebellion.' He had plenty of scope for self-
aggrandisement and coat-turning during the anarchic era
1135–54 when Henry's nephew, Stephen, and his daughter,
Matilda, were contending for the throne. Hurrying back from
Rouen, where he had been attending the dying King, Hugh
convinced the Archbishop of Canterbury that Henry, on his
deathbed, had nominated Stephen as his heir. He did this
because he saw in Stephen a weak man who could be manipu-
lated by the barons. As soon as his expectations were proved
unfounded Bigod raised the standard of revolt at Norwich.
There he was besieged by the King and forced to surrender.
With more charity than wisdom Stephen pardoned the troublesome baron. By 1140 Bigod had declared for Matilda and ral-
lied his forces in East Anglia to fight on her behalf. He felt very
sure of himself, and particularly of the security of his power
base. He had constructed two very formidable castles at Framlingham and Bungay. Indeed, it was his boast that the latter
was impregnable, as the old ballad relates:

> The King has sent for Bigod bold
> In Essex whereat he lay,
> But Lord Bigod laughed at his Poursuivant,
> And stoutly thus did say,

'Were I in my castle of Bungay,
Upon the River Waveney,
I would not care for the King of Cockney.'

We need not follow Hugh Bigod's twinings and tergiversations during the next few years. The accession of a new king, Henry II, did not divert him into the paths of loyalty. Royal and rebel armies made many appearances in the fields and heaths of Suffolk until the final showdown in the summer of 1174. By 1165 Hugh's position was unassailable. Whoever might wear the crown in London, the Bigods ruled Suffolk.

But brilliant, ruthless, mercurial, unpredictable Henry II was not the man to let anyone defy him indefinitely – not a Becket and certainly not a Bigod. Moreover he was a brilliant strategist. Over a period of years, and despite his many preoccupations with his continental dominions, he steadily and stealthily hemmed the troublesome earl (Bigod had been created Earl of Norfolk in 1135) into the corner of north-east Suffolk. He secured control of Norwich and gave the stewardship of Eye castle to a trusted follower. Thetford and Walton were also in royal hands. Henry's master stroke was the building of a fortress whose construction embodied all the latest techniques of military architecture. Orford Castle, best preserved and most imposing of all the medieval strongholds, guarded the sea approaches to Bigod territory (for Orford was then a thriving port) and was only a short march from Framlingham.

It was only a matter of time before Bigod tried to break out of the cordon of royal control. The situation was resolved in two brief campaigns in 1173 and 1174. Hugh combined forces with a detachment of French and Flemish mercenaries. Together they set off from Framlingham towards Bury St Edmunds and Cambridge. They overthrew the royal fortress at Haughley, held by Ranule de Broc, and made their leisurely way westwards commandering food and committing many outrages in the villages and farms along the way. Peasants and freemen fled before the foreigners' advance and watched angrily from a safe

distance as their barns were looted and their animals slaughtered. The indignant Suffolkers were soon to have their
revenge. A mile north of Bury St Edmunds the rebels were surprised by a detachment of royal troops as they crossed the Lark
near Fornham All Saints. Led by Henry's Justiciar, Richard de
Lucy, the King's men scattered the enemy among the low-lying
meadows and marshes. As they floundered up to their knees in
mud and sodden grass they found themselves faced not only by
professional soldiers but by angry countrymen armed with
pitchforks and flails. Many died slowly and hideously that day
besides the tranquil Lark.

Hugh Bigod was not one of them. He agreed to a truce and
the noose around him grew tighter. More royal troops were
stationed in Bury and Ipswich. When the next campaign season opened Hugh Bigod made his last desperate bid for independence. He bought more mercenaries and tried to capture
first Norwich, then Dunwich. Now Henry entered Suffolk in
person and led his army straight to Framlingham. The arrog-
ant earl who had prided himself on the impregnability of his
fortresses declined to put his boast to the test. He surrendered
and agreed to the dismantling of his castles. Framlingham was,
indeed, destroyed and the royal engineers began work on Bungay, driving a mine gallery under the south-west angle of the
keep. But Bigod could not bear to lose his principal fortress and
bought the King off. The ballad writer described the event most
graphically:

> Sir Hugh took three score sacks of gold
> And flung them over the wall,
> Says, 'Go your ways, in the Devil's name,
> Yourself and your merry men all;
> But leave me my castle of Bungay,
> Upon the River Waveney,
> And I'll pay my shot to the King of Cockney'.

But the kings of England had not heard the last of the Bigod
clan. The next earl, Roger, redeemed Framlingham from an
impoverished Richard the Lion Heart and rebuilt the castle on

a more massive scale than its precursor. Caen stone was brought up the Alde, tons of local flint were commandeered and the river Ore was dammed to form a marsh which augmented the defence system on the western side. The new castle was formidable indeed – within a 3000-foot circumference, walled and moated outer bailey, stood an inner bailey itself moated and contained within a 44-foot high wall set with towers, and within that again there was the massive keep of the Bigods. To the west of the inner bailey there was a lower bailey or base court. Today only the inner bailey wall and the dry moats remain but they are impressive enough. In its medieval prime the fortress must have provided a secure bastion for the lord, his family, retainers, animals and a considerable body of armed men. Adequately provisioned, the Bigods could have defied a besieging army for a long time.

Framlingham Castle was finished at about the time King John came to the throne (1199) and soon king and barons were locked in conflict once more. The basic cause of most disagreements between the crown and the leading men of the realm was the issue of power. How absolute was the king? What rights had his subjects? John's exercise of arbitrary rule brought this issue to the fore once more and it became clear to many of the barons that the finding of a permanent solution was now an urgent priority.

That is why 25 barons made their cautious way to Bury St Edmunds in November 1214. Ostensibly they were there to celebrate the feast of St Edmund. In fact they had come to plan concerted action against their liege lord. They discussed the rights and freedoms which it seemed were theirs by natural law or ancient custom. Their discussions were not profound but they were immensely significant, for they were the first gropings towards a political philosophy. They wrote down (or, rather, one of the monks wrote down) a list of liberties and laws for presentation to King John. Then 'they all swore on the great altar that if the king refused to grant these liberties and laws, they themselves would withdraw their allegiance to him, and make war upon him till he should, by a charter under his own seal, confirm to them everything they required.' This was the first draft of the document known as Magna Carta and sealed by a reluctant King John at Runnymede seven months later. Thus can Bury St Edmunds justly claim to be, as the motto on its armorial bearings does claim, 'the shrine of a king and the cradle of the law'. For what was established on that autumn day in 1214 was (as the great judge, Henry Bracton, was soon to state) that 'the King should be under God and the law'.

The participants in this battle of wills were only dimly aware that they were making constitutional history. For them Magna Carta was one stage in a power struggle and they were soon planning the next stage. John mustered his forces in the Midlands. The rebel lords, among whom we are not surprised to find Roger Bigod, levied troops, victualled castles and hired mercenaries. Their power base was London and the eastern counties, and their leader was Geoffrey de Mandeville, Earl of Essex. The first royal advance into East Anglia was repulsed but in March 1216 John, having subdued the rest of the country, turned his undivided attention on the eastern earls. He marched straight on Framlingham where Roger Bigod, true to family tradition, yielded without a fight. The King went on to capture Ipswich, then turned south for Essex and Kent. Everywhere he went he punished by pillage and looting the subjects who had had little choice but to follow their landlords into rebellion. In the south-east John suffered a serious reverse and was forced to flee westwards. Now it was the turn of the barons to reclaim East Anglia and to punish by pillage and looting the subjects who had had little choice but to return to their royal allegiance. Fortunately Suffolk was spared a third demonstration of vengeance when later that year the fortunes of war brought John eastwards again to demonstrate his mastery and his anger to the people of Norfolk and Lincolnshire. Fortunately, too, the campaign of 1216 was the last medieval campaign on the soil of Suffolk.

The Bigods remained the leading men of Suffolk for almost another century and were, to the last, men of independent spirit. Roger Bigod, fifth Earl of Norfolk, and the last of the line, was one of the leaders of fresh constitutional conflict with the crown during Edwards 1's reign. The last glimpse the chroniclers give us of this turbulent family is of a row between Roger and his King. Edward wanted Bigod to serve on a campaign in Gascony. Bigod declined to hazard himself in an army which Edward was not prepared to lead.

> 'With you, O King, I will gladly go; as belongs to me by hereditary right, I will go in front of the host before your face.'
> 'But without me, you will go with the rest?'
> 'Without you, O King, I am not bound to go, and go I will not.'
> 'By God, Earl, you shall either go or hang!'
> 'By God, King, I will neither go nor hang!'

And Bigod won the day.

The Bigods were not the only leaders of Suffolk society but they were in essential respects typical of all the great Suffolk landowners. The only way to personal wealth in early medieval times was the royal service. Those who attended to the king's wants in military, spiritual or diplomatic matters expected to be rewarded by grants of land. They were then able to rule as kings in their own domains for, although the freeman and the peasant were protected by law from the arbitrary actions of their betters, such sanctions counted for little when it came to a disagreement over land or manorial rights. In 1220 a Suffolk tenant had a grievance against his landlord, a member of the Earl of Oxford's family:

> Roger of Kirtley complains that Henry de Vere came to his house at Mutford [near Lowestoft] by night, on Monday in the first week of Lent, and had a lighted torch of wax carried before him, and broke the door and entered his house and asked where was Roger's daughter, whom Roger had often promised him; and when he could not find her in the house, he entered her chamber and sought her throughout the chamber; but her mother had got her out of the chamber

window; and when he could not find her in the chamber, he went out towards Roger's barn which was full of corn, to wit of barley, and he found the door closed and bolted, and he broke the bolt and door, and entered and sought her every-where; and when he could not find her, he set the torch to the corn, and burnt all the corn and the barn.

Roger was a bold man to seek redress against his overlord in the royal courts; we may be sure that the majority of his neigh-bours, when so used, preferred to suffer in silence. Certainly Roger's resort to litigation did him no good. De Vere did not bother to deny the charges; it was enough for him to establish that Roger was his tenant and that, therefore, the man, his daughter, his house, his barn and the produce of his fields were all subject to the lord of the manor. One shudders to think what vengeance de Vere inflicted on his troublesome tenant after they had been dismissed by the court.

Nor was it only in this life that the great men of the county wielded wealth and power. They erected churches, chantries and noble tombs to house their earthly remains and paid priests to say masses for their souls in perpetuity. That is why we can still look on their faces today. Graved in stone, alabaster and brass, they stare at us in frozen piety from their ancient memor-ials. The finest military brass remaining, and the subject of countless brass-rubbings, is in Acton church to Sir Robert de Bures who died in 1331. Scarcely less impressive are the brasses of Sir George Felbrigg at Playford (1400), Sir William Tend-ring at Stoke-by-Nayland (1408), of Sir William and Lady de Burgate (1409) and Robert Atte Tye at Barsham (1415). Dennington boasts the splendid tomb of Lord Bardolph, one of the heroes of Agincourt, and his wife Joan (c. 1450). At Long Melford we can still capture something of the atmosphere of medieval piety in the secret little Clopton chantry with its tomb of John Clopton (1497).

Vandalism, time and clerical cupidity have robbed us of countless other memorials to the great men of medieval Suffolk. Fortunately the marvellous tombs at Wingfield have been spared, and here we must pause again, for we are in the presence of another Suffolk family great in the affairs of county and of state. The earldom of Suffolk was first created in 1336 for Robert de Ufford, a great landowner in the east of the county and, of course, a close attendant on the king, but the Ufford line failed after only two generations and, in 1385, the title was revived for Michael de la Pole. The de la Poles were not soldier-landowners of Norman stock; they were merchants from Hull. They rose to prominence by the simple expedient of lending money to Edward III. Michael's father had bought land in Suffolk and married his son into the great local family of Wingfield. Michael won the confidence of and soon came to dominate the ten-year old Richard II and used his position to extend and consolidate his Suffolk estates. At Wingfield he built himself an impressive, new, fortified manor house. It still stands and is the oldest castle in England to have been continuously occupied to the present day.

The new Earl did not long enjoy his honours and lands. In 1387 he was hounded out of office by jealous rivals and had to flee to France disguised as a peasant. His son waited eight years before he was allowed to succeed to the title and when he did so he held it for only five weeks. Together with his son he perished during Henry v's French expedition of 1415. The de la Poles were among the small army ('We few, we happy few, we band of brothers') which seized Harfleur. The elder de la Pole died of dysentery a few days later. The third Earl lived only to be one of the few English aristocratic fatalities at the Battle of Agincourt. After the fray his body was boiled so that the flesh could be more easily stripped from the bones, which were returned to Wingfield for burial.

The lands and dignities of Suffolk now passed to the late Earl's nineteen-year-old brother, William. The fourth Earl took a leading role in the faction struggle which broke out at the accession of the infant Henry VI. He worked his way into a position of almost supreme power, engineering a marriage between the King and Margaret of Anjou (believed by many to be his mistress) and dominating the pious, weak-minded Henry. His only strong opponent was Humphrey, Duke of Gloucester. That obstacle disappeared in 1447. De la Pole summoned a parliament to meet at Bury St Edmunds, a town the Earl could pack with his own supporters. When Gloucester arrived he was arrested and confined to his lodgings in North Spital of St Saviours. The following morning the Duke was found dead. Lands, offices and titles were now de la Pole's for the taking and he became the first Duke of Suffolk in the following year.

Drunk with power, de la Pole pursued his own policies, accrued further wealth, harrassed his enemies and was quite open in his contempt for public opinion. Popular feeling was running strongly against him. He was accused of having usurped royal power, committed adultery with the Queen, despoiled innocent men of their possessions, given away valuable continental lands for the sake of peace with France, murdered the Duke of Gloucester, misappropriated government funds and planned to set his own son on the throne. By 1450 his opponents were strong enough to force Suffolk to stand trial. Thanks to royal favour, no worse fate befell him than banishment for five years. This did not satisfy his enemies. Off Calais de la Pole was summoned aboard a royal ship. There after a mock trial he was beheaded by an inexpert sailor who hacked at the Duke's neck with a rusty sword for several seconds before severing it. Shakespeare later made the most of this gruesome scene in *Henry VI, Part II* when he made the ship's captain utter the contemptuous words:

Pool! Sir Pool! lord!
Ay, kennel, puddle, sink; whose filth and dirt
Troubles the silver spring where England drinks.

Those words probably summarize fairly accurately what many of the de la Pole tenants felt about their masters. William's heir, John, was 'the greatest landowner in Suffolk and Norfolk and kept an army of retainers to enforce his will. The Pastons were among those who fell foul of the Duke on more than one occasion. In 1465 de la Pole sent his bully boys to pillage and destroy the Pastons' house at Hellesdon. Margaret Paston reported the incident to her husband and noted:

> There cometh much people daily to wonder thereupon, both of Norwich and of other places, and they speak shamefully thereof. The duke had better than a thousand pound that it had never been done; and ye have the more good will of the people that it is so foully done.

John de la Pole could afford to upset farmers, merchants and peasants. He was married to Elizabeth, the sister of King Edward IV.

At a time when unscrupulous men like the Duke of Suffolk held sway and when feuding, rustling and brigandage were common, householders had to take careful thought for the protection of their families and property. It is not surprising that there are over 500 moated sites throughout the county, on most of which houses still stand. At the upper end of the social scale are fortresses such as Framlingham and Wingfield but a great many are timber-framed farmhouses of quite modest proportions. The majority were probably built on traditional defensive positions occupied continuously or intermittently since Saxon times. As well as providing security they have a good, well-drained base on which to build – an important consideration in clayland areas. That is one reason why they have survived. At their beginning they were solid, functional, cold, dirty and smelly. Time and modern sanitation have mellowed them into picturesque gems and probably the most 'typically Suffolk' items in our architectural treasury. Fine examples are at Columbyne Hall (Stowupland), Cotton Hall, Parham Moat Hall, and Little Wenham Hall, England's oldest brick-built house. It is difficult to see these peaceful, 'romantic' edifices for what they really are – monuments of a dangerous and insecure age.

We are indebted to our medieval forbears for another feature of our architectural heritage. This was the great period of Suffolk church building. The Normans were as muscular and progressive about their Christianity as they were about their conquest and administration of foreign lands. Their settlement

in England was accompanied by a spate of religious foundations, both parish churches and monastic centres. The rule of
the Conqueror and his heirs coincided with a great monastic
revival throughout western civilization. Even so, the number of
new houses for monks and nuns built in Suffolk is remarkable.
By 1200 there were 28 such centres, not counting hospitals and
colleges where small religious communities were permanently
employed in caring for the sick and singing masses respectively.
The fourteenth century saw a boom in the establishment of
friaries, and the founding of yet more abbeys. By the end of the
middle ages there was a total of 76 religious foundations of all
kinds in Suffolk. Benefactions by wealthy patrons made most of
these houses rich and the Church became a considerable landowner, a fact which did not always make for harmonious relationships with the people.

Let me illustrate this from the troubled history of Suffolk's
greatest abbey and, indeed, one of the greatest abbeys in Christendom. The community of Bury St Edmund's Abbey enjoyed
the manorial income from vast estates in six counties, taxation
rights over the town and the Liberty of St Edmund, proceeds
from the large number of parish churches in their gift and the
pious offerings of a never-failing flow of pilgrims to the shrine of
the saint. By 1535 the gross annual income of the Abbey was
reckoned at £2,336 16s. 11d., a figure which would have to be
multiplied by at least 200 to reach anything like a modern equivalent. It was partly because of the growing number of pilgrims
that a large town grew up around the Abbey. Increased population meant more people bound to the monastic community by
manorial ties. Though the townsfolk obviously benefitted from
the tourist trade and from such events as the annual seven-day
fair granted by Henry II, they resented the exactions of the
community. The feudal obligations of the citizens were many
and varied: for every acre of land a man held he had to plough
one rood of the abbot's; the farmer had to move his flocks and
herds on to the abbot's pastures and fallow fields every night to
ensure that they would be well-fertilized; every householder
had to devote one day a year to catching eels at Lakenheath for

the monastic table; most irksome of all, at harvest time the local community had to buckle to and bring in the abbot's sheaves before they could start on their own.

These exactions were no worse than those levied by any other feudal overlord but they seemed worse. As the history of trades unionism amply demonstrates, sense of grievance grows in direct proportion to the size of community experiencing that grievance. The burghers of Bury could and did discuss their common complaints when they met at market and at guild assemblies. And grumbling could easily grow into a determination to take concerted action. What also made the situation worse was that the townspeoples' labour was going to support a small group of monks who lived what seemed to many to be a life of parasitic ease behind the high protective walls of their monastery. Many of the people commuted their feudal service for money payments – 1*d.* to be rid of harvest duties, 1*d.* in lieu of eel catching, etc – but this scarcely eased the situation, for the abbot's bailiff extracted the payment with a scrupulosity that looked like avarice. Nor did he shrink from distraining the goods of those who could not pay.

While the townsfolk grumbled in their urban hovels the monks spent a large part of their income on making their abbey church one of the grandest in Christendom. They began immediately after the Conquest, as the poet-monk John Lydgate tells us:

> A new church he did build,
> Stone brought from Caen out of Normandy
> By the sea, and set up on the strand at Rattlesden,
> And carried forth by land.

It is interesting to envisage heavily laden barges berthed at Rattlesden where now the little Gipping burbles through the village, no more than a trickling stream. The church was virtually finished by 1211, an enormous edifice with two great towers surmounted by spires. Its overall length was 505 feet which makes it larger than most surviving Gothic churches. The conventual buildings were no less lavish and the Abbey's gardens, fishponds, vineyards and arable fields covered many acres. Perhaps an early observer was right when he affirmed that the supremest buildings in Christendom were St Peter's Rome, Cologne Cathedral and Bury St Edmund's Abbey.

Such an opinion would not have impressed the men and women of Bury, who were treated as little better than serfs by their cowled masters. At a time when other large towns were gaining charters incorporating guaranteed rights and freedoms (Ipswich received hers in 1200) Bury's citizens had no say at all in their government. The abbot appointed court officers and aldermen; confirmed the election of bailiffs; taxed the town's merchandise; controlled the market, levying tolls on stallholders and keeping the best sites for the Abbey produce. The bitterness of the townspeople ran deep and expressed itself in occasional attacks on monks, Abbey property and servants. Sometimes there were organized demonstrations aimed at forcing concessions from the abbot but the ecclesiastical establishment always proved too strong.

Matters came to a head in 1327. During a winter of widespread anarchy the Abbey's tenants seized their opportunity. On 15 January, 3,000 armed men broke down the gates, destroyed the sacristy, rifled the treasury, looted the Abbey of documents and precious objects, flogged the monks, imprisoned the prior and some of his colleagues in the Guildhall and forced the Abbot, Richard de Draughton, to sign a charter of liberties granting the town virtual independence (a block and headsman's axe were set before him to help him make up his mind). As soon as he could escape, the abbot reached London and repudiated the charter. This only led to fresh outbreaks of violence throughout the spring and summer. The climax of this terrible year came in October. On Sunday the 18th, the monks made an armed attack on the townspeople during divine service in the parish church. The retaliation of the layfolk was fearful. They rampaged through the monastery and virtually razed it to the ground. Nor did the damage stop there; twenty-two of the abbot's manors were devastated before the sheriff of Norfolk arrived to suppress the revolt.

This was no isolated incident, the responsibility of a few hotheads; it was an expression of a deep-seated desire for independence coupled with a dissatisfaction with the religious establishment, strains in the Suffolk temperament which were to reveal themselves time and again in later centuries. Behind the active insurgents of 1327 there were 20,000 malcontents from every social stratum. After the ringleaders had been hanged or exiled, thirty cartloads of prisoners had to be taken to Norwich for trial and a staggering, impossible fine of £140,000 was imposed. The memory of 1327 never faded from the minds of Bury folk. There was to be more blood let during the next two centuries before Henry VIII closed the monastery and the people of Bury St Edmund's tore down the building with their bare hands.

Suffolk people were as devoted to their parish churches as they were distrustful of their abbeys. There was scarcely a church in the county that did not experience some enlargement, extension or alteration in almost every medieval generation. The Normans, as we have seen, built many churches but there are only a few, such as St Mary, Wissington, where the Norman pattern has survived. Naves were widened to accomodate an increased population. Chancels were extended. Chantry chapels – over 2,000 of them between 1200 and 1530 – were enlarged or incorporated within existing buildings. Ecclesiastical fashion also played its part. In the fifteenth century rood screens and lofts became popular and many parishes installed them, even if it meant raising the height of the nave by adding a clerestory in order to achieve a loftier chancel arch. As succeeding building styles emerged, reflecting new aesthetic tastes and the growing skill of craftsmen, parishioners sought to embellish, or sometimes rebuild, in the prevailing fashion. Thus 'Norman' gave way to 'Early English' which in turn was superseded by 'Decorated'. And in the fifteenth century there appeared that crowning glory of Gothic achievement, the 'Perpendicular' style.

This development could be illustrated by a random choice from among Suffolk's many fine churches. I have chosen St

Mary's, Woolpit. The Saxon church was given to St Edmund's Abbey by Ulfcytel, Earl of East Anglia, and the first Norman abbot had the timber edifice pulled down and a new church built. A member of the community served the village as vicar until about 1264 when the first rector was appointed from among the ranks of the secular clergy. This probably coincided with a growth in population which created the need for a more permanent incumbent. Woolpit boasted many well-to-do farmers and prosperous merchants who, for the well-being of the parish, were organized in two guilds – the Guild of the Nativity of Blessed Mary and the Guild of the Holy Trinity. They were not connected, as urban guilds were, with specific trades, but were more like friendly societies. They collected and distributed alms; they cared for the poor and needy; and they supervised the upkeep of the church fabric. Early in the fourteenth century the guilds, the patron and the rector agreed that Woolpit needed a new church. Preserving little but the foundations of the Norman building, they rebuilt in the prevailing Decorated style using Barnack stone from Leicestershire and good Suffolk oak for the doors and roofs. Now they added side aisles, partly for processional purposes and partly to accomodate two chantry chapels – one in the north aisle dedicated to St James, and the other, on the south side, to Our Lady of Woolpit. Who left the money for these chantries and the priests who served them we do not know but whoever caused the Mary Chapel to be built did a material service to the parish, for the fine statue of the virgin became a famous object of devotion, attracting pilgrims from a wide area. The decoration of the new church was completed with a profusion of stained glass, and a variety of wall paintings covering almost every free surface.

Before another century had passed the parishioners of Woolpit were taking fresh improvements in hand. Spurred on, perhaps, by the Perpendicular splendours of nearby Rattlesden, John Turner, John Watson, John Stevenson and other local worthies subscribed to extensive alterations in the latest style. They installed a magnificently intricate rood screen and loft surmounted by a carved canopy (still in place). This meant raising the height of the nave which now gained a clerestory and a new roof. And what a roof! The superb double hammer beams with their angels which seem all set to flutter down on their spread wings were well illuminated by the new clerestory windows and originally glowed with polychromatic splendour. The north aisle was rebuilt at the same time and, to add the finishing touches to the new church, a beautiful south porch was added with statues of Henry vi and his queen above the doorway.

This continuing passion for building and rebuilding betokens considerable local pride and devotion. It illustrates a considerable talent for united and well-organized effort. It is also proof of enormous wealth. Whence, then, came this wealth? The answer can be stated in one word – wool. At the time of the Domesday survey there were some 80,000 sheep in East Anglia, spread fairly evenly over the whole area. The preceeding century had seen the last major onslaught on the forest so thṭt by the time the Normans came, settlement, and therefore agriculture, was fairly ubiquitous. Every farming community made its own cloth and sold the surplus wool in the local market. To these markets at Bury, Ipswich, Sudbury and elsewhere came merchants from London and from Europe. Throughout the early medieval period wool was Suffolk's most important export and the basis of its considerable prosperity. Suffolk was not alone in this; most English farmers reared sheep. Indeed, compared with prime sheep-rearing centres such as the Welsh border and the Yorkshire moors Suffolk wool was of an inferior quality. When Shropshire fleeces were fetching 14 marks a sack, the Suffolk farmer could only get 4 marks for his. Yet Suffolk was richer than Shropshire. The solution of this apparent paradox lies in the volume of trade. Suffolk farmers and merchants did a brisker business because they were closer to their foreign customers. Most of the buyers came across the North Sea from Germany, the Baltic states and the Low Countries – those very regions with which East Anglians had long and close commercial contacts. The sight of foreign buyers riding eastwards to Ipswich or Dunwich followed by long lines of laden packhorses was a very familiar one to medieval Suffolkers.

Then politics intervened. Not for the first time in our history the government realized that a flourishing private enterprise was a useful milch cow. Edward III levied swingeing taxes on markets and customs duties on ports. In addition he used regulations of the wool trades as an economic weapon in his wars with France. The results were dramatic: English merchants quickly turned to more profitable trade and their foreign colleagues sought more reliable markets. Wool exports, standing at 45,000 sacks in 1350 were halved in thirty years and continued to decline.

In some wool-producing areas the result was catastrophic. In Suffolk it was the opposite. And the reason again lies in the close contact with the continent. The difficulties in the English woollen industry coincided with a decline in the Flemish textile industry and the migration of weavers from their depressed homeland. They sought their fortunes first in places where they had contacts, and many of them came to Suffolk. The drop in wool exports and cloth imports was already invigorating the native cloth industry. The wool was here. The labour was here. The trading network was here. Now the technical expertise of the Flemish master craftsmen was here also. Within a generation Suffolk and Essex and, to a lesser extent, the West Country had taken over as Europe's principal exporters of fine cloth.

The effect was impressive. Suffolk, and particularly southern Suffolk, became a boom area. Insignificant towns and villages like Kersey, Lindsey (which gave their names to types of cloth), Long Melford, Cavendish, Clare and Lavenham were put on the map. Old market centres blossomed into populous, bustling towns – Hadleigh, Ipswich and, especially, Sudbury. Over the county as a whole average wealth increased fourfold in the century after 1350. In the centres of the new industry the growth of personal prosperity was much more marked. Lavenham's assessment for taxation in this period increased to eighteen times its original level. The evidence for much of this wealth is still to be seen in the merchants' half-timbered town houses and guildhalls and, above all, in Suffolk's magnificent 'wool churches'.

The lynchpins of the cloth trade were the entrepreneurs, the clothiers, men like Thomas Spryng of Lavenham who lies in the church to whose building he contributed so heavily – the finest church in the county. The organization of the industry has been well described by Nigel Heard in *Wool: East Anglia's Golden Fleece*. I can do no better than quote his words:

> After shearing, the wool was collected by the servants of the clothier, and taken on packhorses to the warehouse, where it was sorted into various qualities and lengths. The wool was then washed and scoured until it was completely clean. The warehouse floor had to be cleared and the wool was spread out in layers, each of which was soaked in oil before the next tier was place on top. Then the heaps were left to steep until the oil was absorbed and the wool supple enough to be worked properly. It was then baled up again and taken by packhorse to the . . . carders . . . whose task was to interlock the wool still further. For this purpose they used wood, or metal cards: spiked boards, between which the fibres were mixed together into a tight mass . . . Carded . . . wool was then distributed among the cottages of the spinners, who were usually women . . .
>
> Spinning in East Anglia was always somewhat primitive, and the old-fashioned distaff continued to be used long after the West Country had adopted the spinning wheel. This made it extremely difficult for the weavers, who constantly complained that they had to use yarn of varying thickness . . .
>
> The larger, capitalistic clothier in the town had the cloth made up by his own hired weavers, or distributed the yarn among the master weavers, and bought back the finished cloth. Country clothiers would use semi-independent weavers working in their own cottages, but gradually these were reduced to the status of wage earners . . .
>
> After weaving, woollen cloth was taken to be fulled. It was

extremely rare for a clothier in East Anglia to own a fulling mill, and they were usually the property of the town authorities, or a group of clothiers. At Colchester there was a mill at New Hithe, which the town authorities made available to the clothmakers, charging a fee per cloth treated. The 'Old Bay and Say Mill' at Dedham was used as a cloth factory, and the adjacent water mill was used by the local clothiers to full their cloth. The newly woven cloth was first of all soaked in clean water and then well beaten. Sometimes the beating was done by hand using wooden paddles, but normally water power was used, especially as the industry expanded. The felting and thickening treatment was completed by scrubbing the cloth with 'fuller's earth', aluminium oxide, which gave a good texture and began the bleaching. After fulling, the cloth was sent back to the clothier and placed over a wooden frame called a tenter. The ends were fixed on to hooks* in the frame and stretched slightly to bring the cloth back into shape. Fabrics were left on the tenter frame to dry out and finish off the bleaching process.

The cloth was now 'white' and ready for sale, or for dyeing . . . Medieval dyers were able to obtain a great variety of dyes from local sources. The most famous East Anglian example was, of course, saffron, which was grown in huge quantities around Saffron Walden until the eighteenth century. Shades of green and yellow could be obtained from such common plants as onions, privet leaves, nettles, cow parsley, and oak bark. Elderberries, damsons, sloe, elder and privet berries made blues and purples. Red could be extracted from sorrel and yellow ladies-bedstraw, and magenta from dandelions. Black and grey came from the bark of alder, and the yellow iris . . .

The annual export of cloths increased throughout the fifteenth century. However, industrial growth was not steady and there were setbacks. The intermittent upheavals of the Wars of the Roses created difficulties. The earl of Oxford, the duke of

*Thus the phrase 'being on tenterhooks'.

Suffolk and the duke of Norfolk, East Anglia's principal land-owners, were leading figures in the conflict (usually on different sides) and this meant that many of their Suffolk tenants were pressed into fighting for the white rose or the red. But the dynastic struggle which engaged the energies of the nobility had little to do with the real history of Suffolk. That was being woven on the looms of Lavenham, Clare and Sudbury.

The development of trade, the building of castles, the growth of important centres of pilgrimage all contributed to the concentration of population and the growth of towns. As we have seen in the case of Bury St Edmunds, it was impossible for feudal law and custom to apply to urban committees. Towns sought and usually obtained charters which would enable them to control their own affairs.

Ipswich's charter was granted by King John on 25 May 1200. It allowed the burgesses to elect their own representatives, appoint their own officials, levy their own market tolls, and it exempted them from interference by powerful magnates and churchmen. The people of Ipswich lost little time in exercising their rights. On 29 June they congregated in the churchyard of St Mary Tower to discuss the details of their new constitution. Three days later representatives gathered to elect a governing body, which did business for the first time on 13 July. They were industrious and proud, these first city elders. They appointed officers to supervise every aspect of the community's affairs. They debated long on what level of tolls would be reasonable. They decreed that a special book called *le Domesday* should be started which would record all their decisions and laws. One of the first things they decided on was the casting of a town seal – a symbol that Ipswich, as a corporate unity, was the equal of the greatest baron in the land.

4. ACTION AND REACTION

Carved on the south porch of Lavenham church (and also repeated many times throughout the building) are the boar and molet, the heraldic devices of the de Vere family. They remind us that the rebuilding of this magnificent church was begun as a thanksgiving for the victory of Henry Tudor over the last Yorkist king at Bosworth. John de Vere, Earl of Oxford, was Henry's captain-general and largely responsible for the successful outcome of the battle. When the earl returned shortly afterwards to his manor of Lavenham he suggested to the great clothiers and other leading worthies that a splendid new church would be an adequate expression of their gratitude for the new dynasty and the era of peace it was ushering in.

The shrewd merchant community may well have been sceptical about the promise of peace. For half a century Yorkist and Lancastrian factions had chased each other in and out of power. There was little reason to suppose that the latest victor would not in his turn be removed from the throne. But Henry VII was made of sterner stuff. He had the ruthless, clear, commercial mind that the Spryngs and their colleagues respected. He administered his kingdom with cold efficiency and made the most of every conceivable source of royal income, but the severe taxes he imposed were more than offset by the increased trade which resulted from Tudor political stability. The new king reigned for 24 years, established the power of the monarchy, broke the power of the feudal nobility, kept England out of foreign conflicts and passed on a well-filled treasury to his son. He also left close to the throne a Suffolk man who was to dominate affairs of state for most of the next reign.

Thomas Wolsey was born the son of a grazier, a supplier of wool and meat to the clothiers and townsfolk of Ipswich.* He entered the Church and used it as a pathway to royal service. He impressed Henry VIII with his capacity for hard work and his grasp of affairs of state, and the young King was soon happy to leave the irksome tasks of government in Wolsey's hands. The rise and fall of the great Cardinal are a part of national rather than county history but in the midst of his pomp and power Wolsey did not forget his origins. He built a college at Ipswich which, if it had survived his downfall, might have established Ipswich as England's third university city.

King Hal seemed, at seventeen, a paragon among rulers – handsome, athletic and intelligent, as much at home in the debating chamber as the tiltyard. But there were deeper levels in his character and in the character of the nation which promised difficult years ahead. This was the time of the Renaissance. Emancipated scholars with new ideas were challenging accepted beliefs and traditional values. They found allies in a growing number of less educated people who shared their disillusionment with contemporary society though they were not always clear about what they wanted to put in its place.

Most of this discontent centred on the religious establishment and it was strongly represented in Suffolk. We have already seen how this could blaze out in white-hot hatred at Bury St Edmunds, and anti-clericalism was by no means confined to a small area. Many Suffolkers resented the parish priests to whom they paid their tithes and various fees, as they were for the most part men who were not noticeably more virtuous than themselves. The standard of education among the clergy was abysmally low. Many of them could scarcely mumble their way through the Latin services and certainly did not

*A half-timbered house in Silent Street is still claimed as Wolsey's birthplace.

understand what they read. Yet these were the men who performed the miracle of the mass, mediated between God and men and imposed spiritual sanctions on members of their flock.

The independently minded men of Suffolk were not slow to find other beliefs more congenial than those propagated by the Church. Wycliffite heresies took firm root here, as they did throughout East Anglia. In villages and towns throughout the county there were groups of Wycliffites or 'Lollards' who met in secret to study the Bible in English, the well-worn, oft-copied tracts which condemned transubstantiation (the orthodox doctrine of the mass), pilgrimages, veneration of images, relics and other Catholic 'superstitions'. Beccles and Bungay were centres of vigorous Lollardy but there is evidence of at least intermittent activity in Ipswich, Bury, Sudbury and numerous towns and villages along the Essex border. The latter probably drew their inspiration from the Lollard group in Colchester, which was, for more than a century before the Reformation, a persistent centre of heresy. Early in the sixteenth century Suffolk was exposed to fresh blasts of unorthodox doctrine. Cambridge University became the academic centre of the English Reformation and preachers infected by the new doctrines went out from there to spread their beliefs in the towns and villages of East Anglia. The most remarkable was 'Little' Bilney, who impressed many by the simplicity and earnestness of his preaching, enraged the clergy by his denunciation of 'idolatry' and 'superstition' and was eventually burned at Norwich in 1531.

Heresy also reached Suffolk from another direction. The teachings of Luther set Germany alight in the 1520s and rapidly spread throughout northern Europe. One of the principal agents in spreading the new heresy was the international mercantile community. Books by German Protestants and by English heretics in exile were smuggled in bales and barrels and then travelled along the packhorse routes to be eagerly bought by the wealthy clothiers and their friends among the gentry, the yeomen farmers and the merchants. One book in particular – Tyndale's English New Testament – was to make an impact which could only be called revolutionary.

The chronicler of Butley Priory sensed clearly the new influences at work in society:

> This year many dreadful gales, much rain, lightning and thunder, especially in summertime, and at odd times throughout the year; also divers sudden mortal fevers, and the charity of many people grows cold; no love, not the least devotion remains in the people, but rather many false opinions and schisms against the sacraments of the Church.

He wrote in 1534. Within four years his beloved priory had been stripped of all valuables, its lead roof removed, its coloured glass smashed and its deserted walls lay open to the weather, the birds and the seekers of free building material. Henry VIII's attack on the monasteries began in 1535 when royal commissioners made a lightning tour of all religious foundations in order to discover reasons, or excuses, for closure. But the vulnerability of the smaller monasteries had already been displayed by Thomas Wolsey, the Ipswich boy who rose to the highest position in the land. In 1527 the Cardinal was looking for money, building materials and income for his colleges at Oxford and Ipswich. He obtained papal bulls for the suppression of a number of small religious houses whose communities had dwindled in size. Many of them were in his native Suffolk. Thus, for instance, disappeared the priories of Snape and Rumburgh, the Priory of St Peter and St Paul Ipswich and Felixstowe Priory.

The lesson was not lost on the King or on Wolsey's young secretary Thomas Cromwell, whose rise was as rapid as his master's fall. In 1536 all small religious houses were closed down. A few had been shown by the survey to be in a state of decay but the only failing of the majority was that their value was less than £200. Thus the nuns of Campsey Ash and Bungay were turned out, as were the Benedictine monks of Eye along with many more of their brothers and sisters. The dissolution of Leiston Abbey, whose picturesque ruins still provide us with a reminder of former glories, also dates from this time. The dealings of royal agents at the Cistercian Abbey of Sibton shows

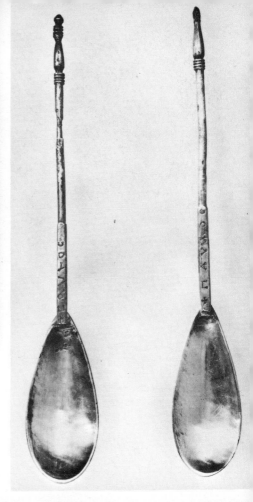

This Bronze Age beaker, found in a burial site near Needham Market, probably dates from c. 1800 B.C.
Some of the magnificent finds at Sutton Hoo.
Silver spoons (probably christening spoons) bearing the legends 'SAUL' and 'PAUL' in Greek.
A gilt bronze winged dragon, originally forming part of a shield. (continued over)

4. Sutton Hoo Treasure: A gold, inlaid buckle of superb, intricate workmanship.
5. A purse lid of bone or ivory with decoration of gold, garnets and glass.

6. (*right*) A 1ft diameter silver salver from the Mildenhall Treasure. The beautiful fourth century raised decoration shows the triumph of Bacchus over Hercules around a central mask of Neptune or Oceanus.

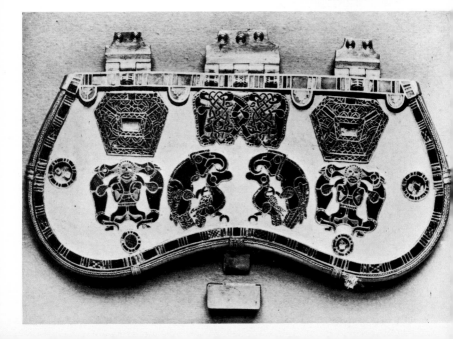

7 & 8. Only the keep of Orford Castle survives today. These reconstructions show what an impressive fortress it was in the fourteenth century. Within its massive walls lay all that was necessary for the material and spiritual wellbeing of a large community.

9. The Plague Stone, Bury St. Edmonds. Originally the base of a cross, this stone was later used as a container for vinegar. Country people visiting the market washed coins in it to prevent infection.

10. (*below*) The whipping post and stocks in the porch of Saxstead Church look picturesque but they are reminders of the cruel public punishments which were staged in every village.

11. (*right*) Jack o' the Clock in Southwold parish church was once part of the striking mechanism of a fifteenth century clock.

12. The de la Poles' impressive castle at Wingfield is probably the only fortified home in England to have been continuously occupied since the 14th century.

13. Poverty and wealth are often reflected in church building. The farming people of Barsham in the Waveney valley added their church to the Norman round tower in the 14th century. After that they could not afford elaborate additions. When the nave needed re-roofing, modest thatch seemed the most economic solution.

14. The rich wool men of Lavenham rebuilt their church almost entirely between 1485 and 1530 in the magnificent, new Perpendicular style. It remains the crowning glory of ecclesiastical architecture in Suffolk.

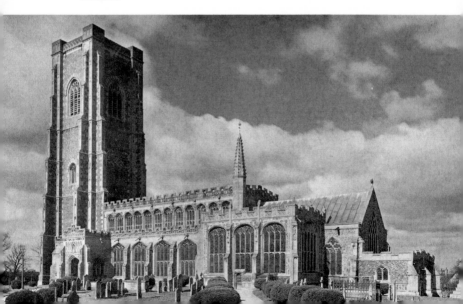

15. Giffords Hall, Wickhambrook, is an excellent sample of a large, fifteenth century moated farmhouse.

16. When, after 1540, the monumental edifice of Bury St. Edmonds Abbey church was left to crumble most of the stone was removed by citizens for their own building projects. Some, however, reversed the process and built their houses into the west front of the Gothic edifice.

17. This superbly executed 16th century monumental brass to the memory of Ipswich merchant Thomas Pownder is of Flemish workmanship. Formerly at St. Mary Quay, Ipswich, it is now on show at Christchurch Museum.

Helmingham Hall, home of the Tollemaches since the 16th century is unique in being the only moated house in England whose drawbridge is still raised every night.

19. Fantistic Ickworth was conceived by Frederick Hervey Earl of Bristol and Bishop of Derry in the 1790s as a monument to the Enlightenment. Unfinished at his death, it lay a mere shell until 1826 when it was completed and decorated in the Regency taste. The Pompeian Room is one of the many elaborate state rooms.

20. (*opposite, top*) Georgian elegance, medieval cosiness and Norman monumentality mingle in Michael Rooker's painting of Bury St. Edmunds as it appeared in the late 18th century. The Church of St. James (now the Cathedral) and the Norman gateway still dominate this part of the city today.

21. (*opposite, bottom*) The motor cars and telegraph poles are the only twentieth century contributions to this corner of medieval Lavenham.

22 & 23. Ipswich benefitted from the commercial boom of the early Victorian era. The discovery of coprolite and the coming of the railway helped the trade of the docks and kept fashionable Ipswich society supplied with its Sundry wants.

24–26. Windmills once dominated every Suffolk skyline. Only a few remain, lovingly preserved or restored. The three types are illustrated here. (24) Buttram's Tower near Woodbridge is a tower mill which was working until 1928. (25) Herringfleet smock mill was used for drainage in the Waveney valley and was rescued from dereliction by the old East Suffolk County Council. (26) Saxstead Green's magnificent post mill is now maintained by the Department of the Environment.

27. The railways brought trade and visitors to the ports. Southwold's fishing fleet (seen here unloading a catch *c.*1908) did brisk business.

28. Lowestoft was the scene of much new building in the late 19th century including a new swing bridge, opened in 1897.

29 & 30. Local ingenuity and skill devised many agricultural machines during the nineteenth century. (29) This grain crusher was made at Stowmarket. (30) This superbly restored, steam-driven thresher dates from *c.*1860.

31 & 32. At the turn of the 20th century the implications of mechanisation were largely unrealised. (31) Bricks were still fashioned by hand in Suffolk's many brickfields like this one at Tuddenham. (32) The Lowestoft fishing industry created a heavy and persistent demand for barrels turned out by skilled coopers.

how many and devious were the methods used to gain possession of monastic property. Thomas Howard, Duke of Norfolk, had designs on the Abbey lands and used his influence to instal William Flatbury as Abbot in 1534. Flatbury acted as representative of Howard and Cromwell in persuading his colleagues to surrender the Abbey in return for assured pensions. Thus, in 1536, although Sibton was worth more than £200 it was surrendered to the Duke.

A rising in the north in protest against religious change having been swiftly put down in 1536, Henry and Cromwell were ready to move against the larger monasteries. Every conceivable pressure was put upon abbots and priors to surrender voluntarily. Early in 1538 the Keeper of the King's Jewels, Sir John Williams, arrived at Bury with a party of workmen. Brushing aside the protestations of the Abbot, they marched into the great church and set to work with picks, hammers and chisels on the shrine of St Edmund. The government had decided that the new religious ideas were right insofar as they complained of the superstitious influences of pilgrimages. At Bury Williams' men had a rewarding though by no means easy task:

> We found a rich shrine which was very cumbrous to deface. We have taken in the said monastery in gold and silver 5,000 marks [i.e. £3,333 in contemporary terms] and above, over and besides a good rich cross with emeralds, as also divers and sundry stones of great value, and yet we have left the church, abbot and convent very well furnished with plate of silver necessary for the same.

This provides us with a good indication of just how wealthy this great abbey was.

By this time royal tactics had proved almost totally successful as far as Suffolk is concerned. The friaries had all disappeared in 1537–8 and of all the ancient monastic establishments, Bury St Edmund's Abbey stood alone. Abbot John Reeve resisted the inevitable until November 1539. Then, in return for an enormous pension (£333 6s. 8d. – the highest

81

granted to any ex-religious superior) he surrendered. He took a house in Crown Street, close by the beautiful and powerful abbey he had ruled for 26 years, and watched the carts rumble past carrying away the Abbey's vestments, silver plate, books, bells and the rolls of lead from the roof, while the crowds of townsmen cheered and then fell upon the ruined buildings to scavenge for neglected treasures and cart away loads of stone for their own use. Reeve was an old man, and the destructive spectacle proved too much for him. On 31 March 1540 he died, never having drawn a penny of his pension. He was buried in the chancel of St Mary's Church, where he remained until 1717 when his place was required for the body of a ship's purser named Sutton.

Most of the newly acquired church lands were disposed of through the Court of Augmentations in the form of grants to royal servants and sales to land speculators and acquisitive landowners. By far the largest beneficiary in this county was Charles Brandon, Duke of Suffolk, whose colourful story we must now tell. His father, William Brandon, who probably hailed from the Breckland town of the same name, had been a staunch Lancastrian, had joined Henry Tudor in exile, fought as his standard bearer at Bosworth and had been killed there when Richard III launched a desperate charge against his rival's position. The grateful Henry took the infant Charles to court and brought him up with his own children, where he became the boon companion of Prince Henry and won the heart of the King's younger daughter, Mary. In 1514, shortly after the execution of the last de la Pole, Henry VIII created his friend Duke of Suffolk. Charles' matrimonial career was almost as chequered as his master's. By this time he had already got into and extricated himself from three marriages. In 1514 he was in Paris as part of Princess Mary's entourage during the celebrations of her wedding to the elderly Louis XII of France. Within 82 days Mary was a widow. Everyone assumed that she would be quickly re-affianced to another member of the French royal house but Mary had other ideas. She made it known that having married once for England's pleasure she would only marry again for her own and that her heart was set on her childhood sweetheart, Charles Brandon.

The couple were married in France and waited there to discover whether Henry's affection was stronger than his indignation. In the Spring of 1515 they were permitted to return. They submitted to the King and received his forgiveness. The marriage lasted 18 years and was a happy one. The ducal couple spent much of their time in Suffolk, and their favourite home was the modest manor house at Westhorpe. Here they entertained all the leading families of the county, the Wingfields, Tollemaches, Drurys, Waldergraves, Heveninghams, Cavendishes, the established gentry and the rising merchants. When Mary died in 1533 she was buried with suitable pomp in the Abbey Church at Bury St Edmunds. At the Dissolution her coffin was re-interred in nearby St Mary's, where a plaque and a window (given by Queen Victoria) still commemorate this royal connection with the county.

Brandon survived his royal wife by 12 years but did not spend them as a widower. He married his 13-year-old ward, Catherine Willoughby, a vivacious, wilful, half-Spanish girl (a relation of the Suffolk Willoughbys of Parham) who grew up to become one of the most remarkable ladies of the Tudor court. Her open support for extreme Protestant views caused her husband much embarrassment, and her sharp tongue often discomfited the pompous prelates who frequented the royal household. Alas, this remarkable lady features little in the story of Suffolk. Henry VIII obliged his friend to exchange most of his Suffolk estates for lands in Lincolnshire and, after 1536, Grimsthorpe in that county became the Brandon's principal seat. But we have not done with the ducal family. The title was inherited in 1545 by Henry, Brandon's elder son by Catherine. Unfortunately he and his brother died of the 'sweating sickness' in 1551. The dukedom now reverted to Brandon's only other child, his daughter Frances by Mary Tudor. Frances also had daughters whose tragic lives were to be bound up with the history of the county and the nation. The name of the elder was Lady Jane Grey.

But before we consider what the ramifications of the Tudor dynastic struggle meant to Suffolk we look again at the day-to-day life of the county where events just as dramatic and momentous were taking place. The middle years of the sixteenth century were tumultuous times. The official publication of the English Bible in 1539 brought religious discord out into the open and, in 1545, the King himself was driven to complain that 'that most precious jewel, the word of God, is disputed, rhymed, sung and jangled in every alehouse and tavern, contrary to the true meaning and doctrine of the same.' Priests and objects of superstition were attacked. Preachers – licensed and unlicensed – wandered from church to church, market to market and from village green to village green, planting new conviction in the hearts of some and confusion in the minds of many.

The dissolution of the monasteries gave rise to the biggest territorial and social upheaval in our history, especially in a prosperous county like Suffolk where there were many men able and willing to compete for monastic land. It was not just church land which came on to the market. The large number of manors, estates and parcels of arable, great and small, gave opportunities for men of all degrees from great magnates to yeomen farmers to exchange, buy and sell property in order to consolidate their holdings. Wealthy London merchants came to live in the county and, like Sir Thomas Kytson at Hengrave, built themselves splendid new houses. Local clothiers also put their wealth into land and thereby bought themselves into the gentry. More and more men and women of this mercantile class were taking a leading role in the life of the county and leaving permanent memorials for themselves – substantial houses such as Gifford's Hall near Sudbury, perpetual charities, and elaborate monuments in brass and stone of which the most splendid is surely the Pownder brass, now housed in Christchurch Mansion, Ipswich.

The shrewd yeoman farmer who could see the drift of the times also grasped the opportunity to consolidate his holdings. This was easier in Suffolk than in some other countries where feudal strip systems had vastly complicated the legal aspects of land tenure. By 1536 many small farmers had, by frugality and a determination to be independent, obtained the freehold of their lands and built up farms which could be simply and efficiently operated. Now they were in a position to add to those farms by purchase, exchange and judicious marriage. An observer early in the next century looked back over recent decades and favourably contrasted the fortunes of the yeomanry with those of some of their more exalted neighbours:

> Continual underliving, saving, and the immunities from the costly changes of these unfaithful times, do make them so to grow with wealth of this world that whilst many of the better sort, as having passed their uttermost period do suffer an utter declination, these only do arise, and do lay such strong, sure and deep foundations, that from thence in time are derived many noble and worthy families.

The history of one such family firmly underlines this opinion. The Bacons were yeoman farmers of Drinkstone and Hesset, two unremarkable villages midway between Bury and Stowmarket. Robert Bacon was also a sheep-reeve for the nearby abbey, that is a man who supervized the shepherds and the flocks in his area. As he could read and write and had a good eye for business, Robert was obviously a cut above his fellows but he was far from being properous. He was, however, able to send his eldest son, Nicholas, to Cambridge and, subsequently, to Gray's Inn to study law. The legal profession had by this time surpassed the Church as the golden road to wealth and preferment, and Robert Bacon was only doing what many of his neighbours did or wished to do. William Drury from nearby Rougham followed the same course, became a leading international legist and returned to build a fine new house in his native village. Thomas Seckford crowned a brilliant legal career when he became Master in Ordinary of the Court of Requests and endowed Woodbridge charities which still pay for the hospital, almshouses, dispensary, lending library and grammar school. William Cordell of Long Melford made so much money out of his posts as Solicitor-General and Master of the Rolls that he could build the magnificent Hall, which now attracts thousands of admiring visitors every year. Queen Elizabeth was entertained there in 1578:

> There were 200 young gentlemen clad all in white velvet, and 300 of the graver sort clad all in black velvet coats and with fair chains . . . with 1500 serving men all on horseback, well and bravely mounted, to receive the Queen's Highness into Suffolk . . . and there was in Suffolk such sumptuous feast-ings and banquets as seldom in any part of the world there hath been seen before. The Master of the Rolls, Sir William Cordell, was the first that began this great feasting at his house of Melford, and did light such a candle to the rest of the shire that they were glad, bountifully and frankly, to follow the same example.

But to get back to Nicholas Bacon. He excelled in his studies and, to further his career, sought the patronage of some great man of the court. He was fortunate in coming to the attention of the greatest man at court next to the King, Thomas Cromwell. The minister was looking for young lawyers of Protestant incli-nations to help in the mammoth task of dismantling medieval Christendom. In 1537 Bacon was appointed a solicitor in the Court of Augmentations. Here, he was ideally placed to take part in the scramble for monastic land and he soon acquired a group of manors around Redgrave, and the Hospital of St Saviour's in Bury. This institution, which had for centuries provided refuge and relief for many aged and infirm people was earmarked by the rising lawyer as a source of stone and timber for the new house he was planning. Work began on Redgrave Hall in 1545 and was completed ten years later, at a cost of £1300. Bacon remained in various government posts through the troubled reigns of Edward vi and Mary and was appointed Lord Keeper of the Great Seal by Elizabeth. Increasing wealth and a marriage into the East Anglian merchant family of Fer-neley enabled him to add to his Suffolk estates and to build himself an even more splendid house at Gorhambury,

Hertfordshire. His son acquired land near Bury and built himself, at Culford, another imposing residence. By the time of Nicholas' death in 1579 the Bacons were among the leading landowners in East Anglia.

The sixteenth century was a good time for the talented, the opportunist and the fortunate; for others it was disastrous. We have not yet mentioned the most potent force in the life of Tudor men and women. It was further reaching in its effects than religious and territorial change and its name was inflation. During the century 1500–1600 the cost of living rose by over 500 per cent, a situation unheard of until our own day. The reasons for this price rise were varied and complex. They still furnish grounds for argument among modern economic historians and were certainly not understood by contemporaries. But they could see the effects:

> . . . the people are increased and ground for ploughs doth want [i.e. 'is lacking'], corn and all other victual is scant, many strangers suffered i.e. 'allowed' here, which make the corn and victual dear. People would labour if they knew where . . . The husbandman would be glad to have ground to set his plough to work if he knew where.
>
> Seeing that wool is dear, cloth must needs rise of price accordingly. And what can be cheap when victual and cloth is dear? Surely nothing that is wrought or made by man's hand or labour, for victual and cloth be the most principal things.

It is inevitably the weakest that go to the wall in times of economic difficulty, as a direct consequence of more powerful groups protecting themselves. Landowners, especially the new men who felt no responsibility to old, feudal tenants, consolidated their estates, put as much land as possible to plough or stock and employed the minimum number of agricultural labourers. In a county like Suffolk which knew the importance of wool it is not surprising that sheep farming predominated. Big landowners found it more economical to turn whole estates over to sheep, and flocks of 2000 or 3000 were quite common.

This often involved the enclosure of land which had previously had other uses, such as common grazing for the local community. More modest farmers followed the same pattern wherever they could: 'clothiers dwell in great farms abroad in the country, having houses with commodities like unto gentlemen,' but all the lands are put to pasture, 'taking thereby away the livings of the poor husbandmen and graziers'. Enclosure was not the only offence committed by the new landlords in the eyes of the common people:

> These raging rents must be looked upon,
> And brought unto the old accustomed rent,
> As they were let at forty years agone;
> Then shall be plenty and most content.

Nor was disaffection restricted to the agricultural scene. The entrepreneurs of the cloth industry, faced with the rising price of their raw material, as well as increased market and shipping costs, attempted to rationalize their commercial activities. Complaints such as the following became common:

> For the rich men, the clothiers, be concluded and agreed among themselves to hold and pay one price for weaving, which price is too little to sustain households upon, working night and day, holiday and weekday, and many weavers are therefore reduced to the position of servants.

The position of weavers, spinners and finishers alike deteriorated through the middle years of the century; most lost whatever independence they had had and were reduced to the level of wage-earners. What made them even more bitter was the spasmodic immigration of foreign craftsmen – Flemmings and, later, Hugenots fleeing from Catholic persecution.

Competition from aliens, high rents, high prices, low wages, debased coinage, confiscation of common land, and unsympathetic landlords – all these grievances combined to drive the poor people of Suffolk to the brink of revolution. The crisis came in 1549 when Robert Ket led a revolt in Norfolk. Many men of the Beccles-Bungay area joined Ket's host on Dussindale Heath outside Norwich where they were eventually cut down by the King's German mercenaries. The rising would certainly have spread back through Suffolk and Essex had it not been for the prompt action of the local gentry. At the first sign of trouble Sir Anthony Wingfield and other J.P.s confronted the disorganized malcontents and arrested their leaders. Two were sent to London for trial and one of them ended his days at Tyburn. The others escaped with the loss of an ear, or a spell in the pillory at Ipswich.

The genuine grievances of the poor and the inadequacy, not to say brutality, of the government in dealing with them stirred up an intense class hatred. The man upon whom feeling was focussed was John Dudley, Duke of Northumberland, the *de facto* ruler of England from 1549 to 1553, during the minority of Edward VI. When, in July 1553, the boy king died and Northumberland tried to exclude his sister, Mary, from the succession by setting Lady Jane Grey on the throne, the commons of England were almost unanimous in rejecting the Duke and his protegé. And the people of Suffolk soon had an opportunity to demonstrate their feelings in a practical way.

Mary was at Hunsdon, near Hertford, when the news broke. She moved away northwards and was on the Cambridge road when a messenger from London caught up with her demanding her return to the capital and advising her that the East Anglian ports had been blocked, rendering escape impossible. Mary continued her journey, lodged briefly at Sawston Hall (south of Cambridge), where she narrowly escaped her pursuers, then entered Suffolk. All along the road men and women left their fields and kitchens, some to cheer and gaze, others to fall in behind the Princess' retinue. Nor was it only the common people who flocked to Mary's support; many of the leading gentry – the Cornwallises, Bedingfields and Jernegans – came to kneel in fealty before her. At Bury she received a royal reception but Northumberland's forces were already on the road and she could not feel safe there. She made her temporary headquarters at the Duke of Norfolk's house at Kenninghall near Thetford. Emboldened by her growing support Mary proclaimed herself Queen and summoned all the local gentry to come to her aid with men and arms.

By the time she set out for Framlingham on 14 July, Suffolk had committed itself. A sizeable army encamped around the ancient fortress under the leadership of the Sheriff, Sir Thomas Cornwallis, Sir William Drury and Sir William Waldegrave. Two days later Northumberland's men, who had reached Cambridge, heard rumours that Mary commanded 30,000 men. It was their refusal to advance against the Suffolk host which sealed the Duke's fate. The Queen selected a council from among her adherents, emptied the prisons to swell her army, and secured the support of the main towns and the east coast ports. These precautions were unnecessary; all opposition collapsed totally and swiftly. When Mary Tudor made her slow way through Suffolk and Essex a few days later it was at the head of a triumphant procession, not a cautious army. Towns and villages poured forth their cheering inhabitants to welcome the rightful heir to the throne who would heed their petitions and deliver them from the anarchic government of self-seeking landlords.

The honeymoon was short-lived. Disillusionment and hatred soon set in. There were no great changes; the old landlords remained in power; the clothiers continued to keep as large a gap as possible between wages and prices; destitution and vagabondage increased. And added to all these ills was a religious persecution of unparalled savagery. The examinations and imprisonments began in 1554. Parish clergy were expelled from livings for refusing to reinstate 'popish' ceremonies. Women were encouraged to give evidence against their neighbours. Houses were searched for Protestant books. Heretics were cajoled, bullied, threatened and bribed into submission and recantation. But there were those who would not recant and in February 1555 the burning started.

Among the first to suffer martyrdom was Dr Rowland Taylor, the burly, much-loved incumbent of Hadleigh. Ever since the time of Little Bilney, and perhaps before, Hadleigh had been an important centre of Protestantism. Taylor was appointed rector in 1544 and his ministry was a fruitful one. Many of his parishioners,

> became exceedingly well learned in the holy Scriptures, as well women as men, so that a man might have found among them many that had often read the whole Bible through, and that could have said a great sort of St Paul's epistles by heart, and very well and readily have given a godly, learned sentence in any matter of controversy. Their children and servants were also brought up and trained so diligently in the right knowledge of God's word, that the whole town seemed rather a university of the learned, than a town of cloth-making or labouring people.

Taylor was openly hostile to the religious policy of Mary's government and because of his fame and popularity many Suffolk and Essex people paid heed to what he said. When the bishop sent a priest to say mass in Taylor's church the poor man was sent packing. Such defiance could not be tolerated. Taylor was hailed off to London and subjected to repeated trials and examinations. He defended himself with cheerful gusto, staunchly refusing to recant. He was condemned to the stake and solemnly degraded from his orders. Or at least, Bishop Bonner of London tried to be solemn. The effect was spoiled when he came to that part of the ceremony at which he was supposed to strike Taylor on the chest with his crozier. 'My lord, strike him not,' cried the bishop's chaplain, noting the heretic's bulk and the defiant gleam in his eye, 'for he will sure strike again.' 'Yes, by St Peter will I,' relied Taylor. 'The cause is Christ's, and I were no good Christian, if I would not fight in my master's quarrel.'

Taylor was brought back to Hadleigh for his execution. Crowds of supporters thronged the town to have a last glimpse of their pastor and encourage him in his ordeal. Only with difficulty did the sheriff and his men succeed in carrying out their grisly task. The first Suffolk martyr perished on Aldham Common on 9 February. A stone monument now marks the spot. He was the first of eighteen men and women in the county who were prepared to die for their faith. How many more suffered ill treatment, harassment and torture we do not know. Nor do we know how many were protected by neighbours and even officials who did not share their beliefs yet were not prepared to lend their support to the English Inquisition.

At last, in November 1556, it was all over. Mary was dead. She was succeeded by Henry viii's last surviving child, the greatest of all the Tudors. Queeen Elizabeth made her first progress through Suffolk in 1561 being sumptuously entertained by the Tylneys, Waldegraves, Tollemaches and other leaders of society. The civic dignitaries of Ipswich also laid on lavish entertainment for their sovereign. But Elizabeth's stay in the city was not an altogether happy one. For a start she was indignant at the behaviour of the local clergy. The extreme Protestantism which had taken root in Henry viii's reign had been nourished with the blood of the martyrs and had now grown into a strident Puritanism. Clergy refused to wear the surplice, were dissatisfied with the 'remnants of popery' in the Anglican services and disliked the Prayer Book. Angrily, Elizabeth ordered them to conform. Some of them did so, outwardly, but royal fiat was powerless to stamp out Suffolk non-conformity.

The Queen was also upset to discover misbehaviour in her own retinue. One of her maids of honour was Catherine Grey, sister of the unfortunate 'nine days queen' and the only surviving grandchild of Charles Brandon and Princess Mary. By the terms of Henry viii's will this 23-year-old girl would automatically become queen if Elizabeth died childless. She was therefore the unhappy and unwilling centre of many plots against the Queen. She had to be very circumspect in all her actions and she was certainly not free to marry at her pleasure. But this is exactly what Catherine had done. She had fallen in love with Edward Seymour, Earl of Hertford, and eight months before the couple had been secretly married. Inevitably Catherine soon found herself in a condition which it would be impossible to conceal indefinitely. It was while the court was at Ipswich that the news was broken to the Queen. Having resigned herself to a permanent virginity Elizabeth could never tolerate the 'lapses' of others. Her treatment of the young lovers borders on the barbaric. They were sent to the Tower; the marriage was set aside; Catherine was forbidden ever to see her husband and to make sure that this rule was obeyed the poor girl was honourably confined in the homes of a succession of East Anglian gentlemen. She pined for her lover, took no interest in her food, no care for her health and in the winter of 1568 she died in Sir Owen Hopton's house at Yoxford.

Religious unrest continued throughout Elizabeth's reign. As the government pursued its *media via*, extremists at both ends of the ecclesiastical spectrum were periodically pressed to conform. A number of Catholics were fined and imprisoned but in our county Puritanism was a much greater problem. Parish clergy and unlicensed preachers stirred the people against all religion that was not 'pure'. The Bishop of Norwich and his officers hailed offenders before the magistrates only to find, on many occasions, that the J.P.s were sympathetic to the accused. Many of the leading families – for example, the Bacons, Jermyns and Highams – were Puritans. They financed preachers, appointed radical clergy to the livings in their gift and opened their houses for separatist meetings. Puritanism thus went from strength to strength. Soon it was a matter not merely of isolated believers and congregations, but of an organized party. In 1582 there came, 'three score ministers, appointed out of Essex, Cambridgeshire and Norfolk to meet the eighth of May at Cockfield, there to confer of the Common Book, what might be tolerated, and what necessarily to be refused in every point of it; apparel, matter, form, days, fasting, injunctions, etc.' The rector of Cockfield, John Knewstub, was a leading figure among the Puritans in West Suffolk but he had his counterparts in such important centres as Hadleigh, Ipswich and Beccles.

Religious squabbles and the constant fear of social unrest arising out of the nation's continuing economic difficulties, were the only matters that deflected the solid gentlemen, yeomen and burghers of Suffolk from the major problems of crops, stock thefts and trade. These were the golden years of the

Elizabethan age – the years of Shakespeare, Drake and Raleigh – but the letters and reports from Suffolk are filled with rumours of pirates off Lowestoft, of merchants illegally shipping timber and grain to the continent, of the Whitsun plays at Hadleigh being cancelled because 'disordered people of the common sort are apt to misdemean themselves.' Even the Armada threat of 1588 failed to strike much of a patriotic fire in Suffolk. The decayed coastal defences had to be hurriedly repaired. When the eastern ports were required to provide a quota of ships for the royal fleet they all pleaded poverty. The Spanish wars had already caused them severe loss of trade, they argued, and they could only furnish a fraction of the required shipping. When the time came for the county levies to assemble at Tilbury the men of Suffolk had to be cajoled again for they were reluctant to leave their farms at harvest time and even more reluctant to leave their own county.

Yet there is one Suffolk name which ranks alongside those of the great Elizabethan adventurers. Thomas Cavendish of Trimley St Martin proved that Devon had no monopoly of mariners and that 'wet and cold cannot make them shrink nor strain whom the North Sea hath dyed in grain.' He was one of the many sea dogs who served his Queen and his own pocket by harassing Spanish shipping and settlements in the Americas. In 1586 he decided to emulate Drake's great exploit of circumnavigating the globe. Setting out in the summer with three ships, he completed the incredible journey in a little over two years. In 1591 he set out to repeat the venture and to open up commerical relations with the Orient but, worn down by storms and disease, he died off the coast of Brazil and was buried at sea.

5. KING AND PARLIAMENT

The beginning of the seventeenth century found the cloth trade, on which so much of Suffolk's prosperity rested, in a state of decline, or rather of transition. What came to be called the 'old draperies' were giving way to the 'new draperies'. The old system had been badly hit by market changes, new techniques and the growth of monopoly.

The long war with Spain, involving, as it did, the disruption of trade with the Spanish Netherlands, was an important cause of decline. Another was the development of new markets. The Portuguese, followed later by the Dutch and the English, opened up trade with the Orient. The establishment of a policy of detente with the Ottoman Empire eased the way for commerce with the Levant. The planting of European colonies in Africa and the Americas provided captive markets for the goods of the Old World. But the requirements of these new consumers were not the same as those of England's old trading partners. In particular, the inhabitants of tropical and sub-tropical lands did not want to drape themselves in heavy Suffolk broadcloth.

These commercial complications were a challenge and one to which the Suffolk clothiers would probably have responded if they had been left to their own devices. But the cloth trade was of national importance; East Anglia was not the only production area involved. Governments and powerful mercantile groups tried to find national solutions to the new problems. Area specialization was seen as one means of rationalizing the industry. Fulling could be more efficiently and cheaply carried out in counties like Yorkshire where there was abundant water power. Thus, within a few decades, Suffolk's small-scale fulling industry dwindled and many craftsmen travelled north to find work.

This was possible because of the growing control of the East Anglian industry exercised by London merchants, most of whom belonged to companies such as the Merchant Adventurers, the Muscovy Company and the Eastlands Company which had official or unofficial monopolies in large trading areas abroad. These men could outbid the local clothiers for yarn and could afford to pay more for unfinished cloth than the exporters of Ipswich and Colchester. Suffolk clothiers who tried to break the monopolies often found themselves prosecuted in the capital by London businessmen who were supported by a growing volume of legislation. The disappearance of free trade meant that Suffolk clothiers, who best knew their own business, were hampered in their activities, with inevitable results:

> The decayed state of this poor corner [derives] chiefly, if we be rightly informed, by restraint made by a statute prohibiting that no Suffolk cloths should be transported, and not here dressed before they are embarked, thereby changing the accustomed gainful trade . . . with such cloths as were best saleable in Spain and now through long want of access into those parts we find the stocks and wealth of the inhabitants greatly decayed.

Such was the claim made by the merchants of Ipswich in 1588 and the situation did not improve during the next four decades. A complaint made by the Suffolk magistrates in 1619 shows one result of an enforced reliance of London merchants:

> Not many years since (they say) our country tasted of an extraordinary calamity in the breaking of one Cragg, a merchant beyond the seas, by occasion whereof diverse merchants in London, bankrupting likewise, overthrew the

estates of divers clothiers in our country . . . And this loss not yet recovered . . . one Gerrard Reade, a merchant of London, having gotten of the clothiers estates about £20,000 into his hands for cloths bought of them doth now withdraw himself into his house and hath set over his goods unto his friends, answering the said clothiers that he is able to make them no satisfaction. There are fourscore clothiers of Suffolk at the least to whom he is indebted . . . and their people being 5,000 at the least that work unto them, they will be brought into such extremities that neither the clothiers by their trade nor we by any means we can use shall be able to relieve them.

Three years later the same justices reported to the Privy Council that the bankruptcies were continuing, the clothiers of 20 towns having on their hands 4,453 broadcloths worth £39,282.

The clothiers and their allies took both negative and positive action to try to remedy this situation. In a negative, reactionary spirit they banded together in an attempt to create strong, local organizations capable of resisting outside pressures. A company of clothworkers founded at Ipswich in 1590 had as its avowed intentions that 'the said mysteries and sciences may be better ordered, the town better maintained, and the country near about it more preferred and advance'. A similar organization was founded at Bury in 1607. They totally failed in their object of protecting local trade from the tycoons of London. What they did achieve was to enable the clothiers to restrict the wages of and impose strict conditions upon the craftsmen who were already experiencing considerable hardship. The East Anglian clothmen also tried to check the import of new, lightweight cloths from the Low Countries but the Dutch had come up with a fabric which, while warm, was easier to work and lighter to wear and its popularity was irresistible. This head-in-the-sand attitude was not calculated to revive the English industry, and many Suffolk craftsmen, driven by economic hardship and religious persecution, were forced to emigrate to the Netherlands.

But some craftsmen had long since taken a more positive line and one that was to preserve the Suffolk clothmaking industry for another century. Copying the skills of immigrant Dutch workers, they had turned their attention to the spinning of yarn and the weaving of new draperies. These new cloths went under such evocative names as 'fustian', 'bay', 'say', and 'stuff'. The Suffolk centre of the new draperies was Sudbury but the spinning of yarn (a process known as 'kembing') was more widespread. In the early years the spinners were independent and made their own arrangements for selling the yarn in London or Norfolk, but before long capitalist entrepreneurs had interposed themselves and taken over the organization of the industry. Thus did the woollen industry manage to keep on its feet until the disruption caused by the Civil War.

The solid Puritan majority in Suffolk left little room for doubt about which side the county would espouse in the conflict between King and Parliament. In fact, no other shire was less divided in its allegiance. All England suffered under the harsh taxes and despotic rule of the first two Stuarts but grievance was more sharply felt in Suffolk, where many people could still remember the prosperous times. Things had certainly changed for the worse since then, as taxation figures show. For Elizabeth, Suffolk could raise a subsidy of £6,828; by James' times the assessment had fallen to £2,137. Most Suffolkers felt that this money was going to support a government which did nothing for them and whose policies they could not support. The Elizabethan poor law, which reached its final form in 1601, made the parish responsible for all of its inhabitants unable to care for themselves. Throughout the county the number of those in need of relief rose and the poor rate rose with it. The magistrates heard frequent pleas for leniency from overseers and churchwardens who simply could not collect the necessary money. When they relayed these appeals to the Privy Council they were simply ordered to get on with their jobs because the growing evil of vagrancy had to be brought under control. Such cold comfort only added to the bitterness felt by a generation of Suffolk gentlemen who remembered the Armada and were disgusted by the policy of rapprochement with Spain being pursued by King James.

The inhabitants of the coast had more reason than most to feel aggrieved with the government. Fishing, shipbuilding and coastal trade had for years been thriving activities. Two hundred or more ships out of the ports of Lowestoft, Southwold, Walberswick, Dunwich, Aldeborough and Orford plied the North Sea herring grounds and the Icelandic cod fields throughout most of the sixteenth century. In 1572 the above-mentioned ports together with Ipswich and Woodbridge owned 146 coastal trade vessels, which carried cloth, oil, flax, hemp and wine across the Narrow Seas and plied along the coast with timber, fuller's earth, hides and Newcastle coal. The growth of maritime enterprise in the sixteenth century brought prosperity to the shipyards of Ipswich and Woodbridge. In the early years of the century Ipswich was the principal supplier of large merchant ships to London, and thousands of Suffolk oaks went into a succession of fine vessels. Woodbridge was always a close rival of the neighbouring port but Ipswich added to its prosperity by its production of the nation's finest cordage and sail canvas. The turn of the century saw business booming and a succession of fine ships being laid down – the *Matthew* (320 tons) in 1598, the *Elbing Bonaventure* (300 tons) in 1599, and the *Providence* (300 tons) in 1603. The trend continued and in 1618 we find the East India Company placing an order for a ship of 500–600 tons.

But, if the metaphor is not an obvious one, the tide had already turned. The principal villain was the sea itself, which attacked most of the east coast ports but especially Dunwich.

> The Queen's majesty's town of Dunwich is by the rage and surges of the sea, daily wasted and devoured; and the haven of her highness said town by divers rages of winds continually landed [i.e. silted] and barred, so as no ships or boats can either in or out, to the utter decay of the said town, which heretofore hath well and faithfully served her majesty and her noble progenitors . . .

That was the situation in 1573 and year by year more houses, churches and streets vanished. The inhabitants lacked the resources and technical skill necessary for the construction of adequate sea defences and, despite frequent pleas, no help was forthcoming from the government. Southwold, also, was fast silting up by 1620 and fishermen could no longer rely on access to the harbour at Walberswick.

Piracy was another problem. It is a crime as old as maritime commerce itself but it became particularly virulent in the North Sea from the late sixteenth century. Operating out of Dunkirk, Ostend, Sluys and Nieuport, the privateers played havoc with coastal and international shipping. In 1596 a small fleet of Dunkirkers blockaded Harwich. In 1602 east coast merchants were forced to adopt a convoy system. In 1619 a national subscription was raised to relieve the people of Dunwich, Southwold and Walberswick whose misfortunes were, in part, blamed on pirates. In 1626 a Dunkirk privateer sailed into Sole Bay at Southwold with guns blazing. While the townsfolk fled from the harbour the pirates cut out a merchant ship and made off with her. Between 1625 and 1627 no less than thirteen Aldeburgh ships of a total value of £6,800 were lost to pirates.

The last major disaster to strike the Suffolk coast was the rapid decline of the shipbuilding industry. Fine ships were built at Ipswich and other Suffolk yards until about 1638. By that time, not only was timber becoming scarce and, therefore, expensive, but the London dockyards were growing, a fact recognized by Henry Johnson of Aldeborough when he left his own declining port and founded the Blackwall Yard on the Thames. The venture soon made him a fortune, encouraged similar enterprises and hammered the final nail into the coffin of the Suffolk industry.

What angered the coast men was that, although the government did virtually nothing to help them in their difficulties, it frequently demanded contributions of men, money and ships towards royal naval expeditions and towards the defence of the realm when disastrous Stuart policies plunged it into senseless war. Time and again the justices reported to the Privy Council that the levies could not be met. Time and again ports petitioned unsuccessfully for payment for ships donated to the national cause. After 1619 local ill-feeling centred on one man, George Villiers, Duke of Buckingham, royal favourite, Lord High Admiral and virtual ruler of England. Many men had cause to hate this smooth, handsome, incompetent courtier on whom both James and his son doted – none more so than John Felton of Pentlow, near Sudbury. A soldier who in the service of his country had lost the use of his left hand, Felton's repeated pleas for military promotion were ignored. At last he obtained an interview with the great Buckingham and explained that without a commission he could not live. 'If you cannot live you will have to hang,' was the favourite's answer. This rebuff tipped the balance of Felton's desperate mind which from this point fed only on thoughts of revenge. On 23 August 1628 he went to Buckingham's rooms in Portsmouth armed with a cheap knife, and while the Duke was surrounded by admirers and petitioners, he struck him down. Felton was fêted throughout the nation as a hero and a deliverer but this could not save him from the gallows. He died in November, knowing that few men of Suffolk had rendered their country better service.

The assassination of Buckingham, like the ship money case and the arrest of five members, was one of the signposts on the road to the great rebellion. It was a symptom, not a cause, of unrest. At the heart of it, in Suffolk at least, was the Stuart attack on the religion espoused by the leading members of the community. Puritanism was powerful in Suffolk because it was an expression of many of the qualities shared by Suffolk men and women – fierce independence, simplicity, dislike of 'fripperies' and pomp, appreciation of the business virtues of common sense and honesty, mistrust of mysticism. In 1604 new canon laws were issued which enforced the use of the existing Prayer Book with all rituals and ceremonies involved in it. Armed with these the bishops carried out sporadic attacks on Puritan clergy. Some resigned their livings, only to be appointed to 'lectureships' by powerful patrons. Others conformed outwardly but continued to preach their predestinarian doctrines. Persecution only increased their influence.

Suffolk pulpits were occupied by some formidable men in those days. The figurehead of the movement was Samuel Ward, town preacher of Ipswich from 1603 to 1635. Forthright yet wise, Ward was widely respected and his sermons at St Mary le Tower attracted large congregations. He was also a familiar figure in Cambridge and London pulpits. Ward was a gifted artist and his political caricatures won him many admirers and not a few enemies. He even passed a few days in prison for lampooning Spanish dignitaries. He published several tracts and sermons which similarly offended the establishment. In 1623 the King wrote personally to the Ipswich corporation asking for Ward's suspension from office – a request which the city fathers declined. In the next generation we find one of the great Puritan writers serving as rector of Lavenham. William Gurnall, though lacking priest's orders, was appointed by the Puritan lord of the manor, Sir Symonds D'Ewes, an action sanctioned by parliament in 1644. During his 33-year incumbency he wrote one of the most famous Puritan devotional works, *The Christian in Complete Armour,* dedicated to 'my dearly beloved friends and neighbours, the inhabitants of Lavenham'.

Another of Suffolk's famous Puritan sons was not a minister. John Winthrop, lord of the manor of Groton, was a landowner descended from a line of Lavenham clothiers, and a practising lawyer. But his conscience would not allow him to enjoy the rural peace of his patrimonial estates. In June 1628 he met with others of like mind in Cambridge and they resolved to get together a party of men and women prepared to follow the example of the Pilgrim Fathers. Winthrop was elected their leader and, less than two years later, he led a fleet of emigrés out of Southampton. Thus was founded the colony of Massachusetts of which John Winthrop was first Governor.

It was the emergence of William Laud as controller of ecclesiastical affairs (he held various bishoprics and became Archbishop of Canterbury in 1633) that precipitated the religious and constitutional crisis. He was determined to enforce conformity by every possible means – using paid informers, muzzling the press, prosecuting Puritan clergy in the courts.

His treatment of the Puritan propagandist Alexander Leighton in 1630 appalled the nation. Convicted in Star Chamber, Leighton was sentenced to be fined £10,000, to have both nostrils slit, both ears cut off and his face branded, to be whipped, pilloried and then imprisoned for life. It is no wonder many Suffolk Puritans took fright. Many of them, led by Dr Dalton of Woolverstone, planned to emigrate to America. They sought Samuel Ward's advice and the patriarch decided there was no dishonour in the younger members fleeing persecution to set up a holy commonwealth in the New World but that those too old for such adventures should remain to resist the tormentors. In 1633, 600 Suffolk men and women sailed from Ipswich and settled in Massachusetts in a place they named after their home town. Two years later Samuel Ward was dismissed from office, and imprisoned. At length he fled to Holland. But he returned to die in Ipswich and to be buried in the church he had served so faithfully. His strangely worded memorial can still be seen:

> Watch Ward! yet a little while,
> And He that shall come, will come.

These were crisis years for Suffolk. Ruined by economic distress and royal taxation, the people were no longer able to meet the unremitting demands made by the government. In 1640 the sheriff, Sir Symonds D'Ewes, was required to collect £8,000 in ship money. He received £200. In the same year 600 soldiers, levied at Bungay for the Scottish war, mutinied and besieged their deputy-lieutenants in one of the town inns. In Ipswich a set of the new canon laws was nailed to the pillory and 16,000 poor people assembled for a march on London to petition Parliament for the redress of grievances. The following year Sir Lionel Tollemache and Sir Thomas Jermyn, the royal commissioners, did not dare to muster the county militia.

As soon as the breach between King and Parliament was opened, the anti-royalists in Suffolk secured their county. They took charge of the Bury powder magazine and the Landguard fort at Ipswich. Where necessary, officials were appointed whose loyalty to Parliament was assured. In February 1643 the

Eastern Association, a union of Essex, Suffolk, Norfolk and Cambridgeshire for mutual defence and the provision of men and money for the war effort, was formed. It was to be the Parliamentarian power base, providing considerable resources for the cause and effectively closing the east coast to Royalist sympathizers. There were a few supporters of King Charles in the county but they were powerless to help him. A few of them made a half-hearted attempt to hold Lowestoft in March 1643 but were soon overpowered.

It was at Bury St Edmunds in January 1645 that Oliver Cromwell summoned a conference to plan the formation of a professional militia – the New Model Army. So far the Parliamentary cause had relied on the half-trained county levies and though these had usually proved more than a match for the King's forces they were always reluctant to fight far from home or permit their military duties to interfere with the demands of their farms and businesses. This was certainly true of the Suffolk men who frequently grumbled about marching to distant parts of the realm. However, Cromwell was only too pleased to call on the Suffolk levies six months later when the Royalists were advancing through the Midlands. He urgently summoned Suffolk's cavalry to muster at Newmarket and the infantry at Bury. Each trooper, he promised, would receive 14s. and each dragoon 10s. 6d. per week. The Suffolk men supported him and helped him to win the great decisive victory at Naseby. The closest that the war came to Suffolk was Colchester which was seized for the King by the Earl of Norwich in 1648. Cromwell was away with the bulk of the army fighting the Scots, and General Fairfax had inadequate forces to take the ·citadel. However, with the aid of Suffolk forces 'Black Tom' was able to cut the town off from all land and river supply routes and, after a siege of two and a half months, Colchester fell.

But Suffolk solidarity for Parliament did not endure. The fate of the King and the growing power of the army, some of whose leaders were religious fanatics, alarmed many people. Like most revolutions, this one did not turn out as everyone had expected. It was one thing to purify religion of superstitious and popish relics; it was quite another to show a total disrespect for the things of God, as did soldiers who used churches for stables and fired their muskets at ancient windows and monuments. The full horror of rule by fanatics was brought home to the county by the activities of two of its own sons, William Dowsing of Laxfield and Matthew Hopkins of Great Wenham.

Dowsing rose from obscurity and returned to it after a brief blaze of what he probably conceived as glory. In August 1643 Parliament decreed that altars, candlesticks, pictures and images were to be removed from churches. Dowsing immediately came forward as one prepared, 'for the zeal of the Lord', to undertake this task and was appointed to the post of Parliamentary Visitor by the General of the Eastern Association. After creating havoc in Cambridgeshire he turned to his own county. Between January and October 1644 he toured Suffolk with a troop of soldiers. He smashed stained glass windows, defaced bench ends and carved fonts, broke down crucifixes, tore up brasses and obliterated inscriptions. In his disastrous rampage he visited 150 churches virtually at random and carefully noted down in a journal the work of destruction. At Clare

> we broke down 1000 pictures superstitious. I broke down 200; 3 of God the Father and 3 of Christ and the Holy Lamb, and 3 of the Holy Ghost like a dove with wings; and the 12 Apostles were carved in wood, on the top of the roof, which we gave order to take down; and 20 cherubims to be taken down; and the sun and moon in the east window, by the King's arms to be taken down.

Some parishes, it is only fair to say, welcomed Dowsing and co-operated with him but others, such as Ufford, put up a show of resistance, locked the church and tried to keep the desecrators at bay. Many churchwardens, even if they were sympathetic to Dowsing, resented having to pay the standard charge of 6s. 8d. for his visitation.

A more sinister figure was Matthew Hopkins, the witch-finder-general. Such a man could only thrive in a troubled time and place where in every community people were divided against each other, where loyalties clashed, where all calamities were put down to supernatural agency, where the dislocation of life patterns had driven many to the brink of mental collapse and where the exponents of an introspective religion held sway. Hopkins became famous after he had uncovered a supposed witches' coven near Manningtree. He was asked by other towns and villages to examine men and women (usually women) suspected of having familiar spirits. For three years he toured Suffolk and neighbouring counties applying his 'tests' and supervising the resulting executions. In that time he hounded to death 106 people in our county.

His method was to apply various spectacular tortures to the accused persons until they confessed. The supposed witches were stripped, stuck with pins, denied food and rest, or made to walk until their feet were cut and blistered. When all else failed they were 'swum'. For this they had their thumbs and toes tied together and were dragged through the local pond in a sheet. If they sank they were innocent. If they floated they were in league with the devil. The 80-year-old vicar of Brandeston was forced to run about until he was breathless for several nights in succession until, in a state of exhaustion, he confessed to being possessed by two imps which caused shipwrecks and other havoc. The poor old man was forced to say his own burial service before being hanged as a wizard. As a contemporary complained,

> Every old woman, with a wrinkled face, a furrowed brow, a hairy lip, a gobber tooth, a squint eye, a squeaking voice, or a scolding tongue, having a ragged coat on her back, a skullcap on her head, a spindle in her hand, and a dog or cat by her side, is not only suspected but pronounced for a witch.

Fortunately, poetic justice caught up with witchfinder-general who was, himself, tried for witchcraft in 1647 and, apparently, hung.

The placing of the county on a military footing was another cause of discontent. Soldiers were billeted on townspeople without payment. They took provisions from shops and homes and ransacked the houses of the gentry for arms and plate. A visit of one Cromwellian troop at Somerleyton House in 1642 cost Sir John Wentworth £44 in various appropriations plus £160 worth of gold. The local militias were expected to train every week and provide their own equipment and the county as a whole had to pay £1250 for the maintenance of the army. All this the people were expected to suffer gladly for the sake of their 'defence'.

Such experiences and the harsh new laws of the Commonwealth transformed the sympathies of many Suffolk people. In 1648 there was a serious riot at Bury when the authorities tried to prevent the hoisting of the maypole. The local arsenal was seized and angry people rushed through the streets shouting, 'For God and King Charles!' The outburst was contained as were similar risings in Aldeburgh and Lowestoft. Suffolk was tired – tired of war, of religious conflict and of political manoeuvrings by army and Parliament. None of them seemed to make any difference – the cloth industry was still declining; the harbours were still silting up; and there were still thousands of people living at bare subsistence level in thatched, rat-infested hovels that would, 300 years later, be regarded as 'quaint' by twentieth-century weekenders.

Centuries later, Suffolk was to play its part in writing a gruesome postscript to the English Revolution. Oliver Cromwell's enemies did not allow his bones to rest in peace. In 1661 the Protector's body was dug up, hung at Tyburn, decapitated and buried at the foot of the gallows. The head was stuck on a pole on Westminster Hall where it rotted gently until it blew down in a gale a quarter of a century later. The grisly relic was retrieved by a soldier and went through many adventures before it came into the hands of a Suffolk family. At length, Canon Wilkinson of Woodbridge, a member of the family, arranged with the fellows of Sydney Sussex, Cambridge (Cromwell's college) that the head should be given decent burial within the precincts. This was done in 1960.

6. LEISURE
AND LETHARGY

The century following the Restoration of the monarchy in 1660 was a time of immense contrasts, even contradictions. The people rejoiced to throw off Puritan restraints and return to their traditional sports and pastimes. At the same time preachers inveighed against the debauchery of the age and Suffolk had more Nonconformist assemblies than most other counties. East Anglia was still the industrial heart of England, yet the new draperies were following the old into decline. The shipyards decreased in importance but Suffolk mariners and men o' war took part in the principal naval actions of the Dutch wars – some off Suffolk's own coast. Poverty, unemployment and vagrancy mounted steadily but more fine houses were built in this period than ever before, and the Age of Enlightenment was reflected in the gracious living of the élite of Bury and Ipswich. The gap between rich and poor was steadily increasing. When England welcomed back Charles II it rejected the 'democratic' experiment of the Commonwealth and declared that it had little interest in moving towards egalitarianism. Now, all men who could do so aped the manners and fashions of the court. When the King visited Newmarket or stayed with the Arlingtons at Euston, local squires and their wives clamoured to see what the ladies and gentlemen of the court were wearing. When burgesses called professionally or socially at the country mansions of the great, they took careful note of what they saw and planned to have copies of the furniture made for their town houses. And the labourer, the out-of-work weaver, the under-paid spinster? They tugged the forelock to all whose charity might temporarily ease the burden of poverty.

The establishment of Newmarket as the home of the sport of kings brought court and county closer than ever before. It all began when James I built a hunting lodge in the town so that he could more easily take advantage of the Heath's excellent hawking and hunting facilities. He and his son both loved the place and Charles I instituted the first cup race in 1634; but it was Charles II who laid the firm foundation of royal patronage. He came to Newmarket almost every spring and autumn to race his horses against those of his courtiers and friends.

> By night we got to Newmarket, where Mr Henry Jermyn lodged me very civilly. We went immediately to court (the King and all the English gallants being here at their annual sports) supped at my Lord Chamberlain's and next day after dinner went on the heath, where I saw the great match run between *Woodcock* and *Flatfoot*, the King's and Mr Eliot's of the Bedchamber, many thousands being spectators . . .
>
> (John Evelyn's Diary)

Royal patronage encouraged courtiers and noblemen to build houses in and around Newmarket. The most magnificent was, beyond a doubt, the mansion which Henry Bennett, Earl of Arlington, erected for himself at Euston. Arlington, having shared with Charles II the hardships of exile returned to share with him the benefits of power. He became Lord Chamberlain and a member of the Cabal, Charles' intimate group of advisers. A man of great taste, he amassed the considerable wealth necessary to enable him to indulge it. Evelyn said of him that he was 'given to no expensive vice but building and to have all things rich, polite and princely'. Euston Hall was, in the diarist's opinion, 'a very noble pile', built in the French style, 'formed of additions to an old house, yet with a vast expense, made not only capable and roomsome, but very magnificent and commodious, as well within as without, nor less splendidly furnished'. There were formal gardens, an orangery, pleasure gardens, a lake and a canal formed by diverting the nearby river. The park, which had a circumference of nine miles, enclosed a herd of 1,000 deer.

Bury St Edmunds shared in the enthusiasm for building which inspired so many people in this new, gracious age. Suffolk gentlemen and well-to-do burgesses erected town houses or built classical facades on to medieval structures. Typical of the townsfolk who had great pride in their young borough (Bury was incorporated in 1606) was Thomas Macro, grocer, alderman and five times chief magistrate. It was he who built the town's most original seventeenth-century dwelling, Cupola House. Macro – whether solely as a result of honest trade we know not – became a very rich man. He acquired the sizeable estate of Little Haugh at Norton. He educated his son, Cox Macro, at Cambridge and at foreign universities. Cox became one of the leading linguists and antiquaries of his day and was able to devote his life to the acquisition of a large library and many fine works of art. He could pay leading continental artists to work on the decoration of his house. Clearly it was not only noblemen who could creatively employ taste and intellect when endowed with the necessary wealth and leisure. Cox Macro was undoubtedly one of the local worthies Daniel Defoe encountered here in 1722. What impressed Defoe about Bury was 'the polite conversation, the affluence and plenty they live in, the sweet air they breathe in, and the pleasant country they have to go about in'.

The pattern of life at Newmarket had become firmly established by Defoe's time. He encountered there

> a great concourse of the nobility and gentry; but they were all so intent, so eager, so busy upon the sharpening of the sport, their wagers and bets, that to me they seemed just so many horse coursers in Smithfield.

Wealthy courtiers and landowners spent large sums of money breeding North African stallions and champion thoroughbreds from Arabia and Turin. Breeding and training establishments began to appear and, because of the fortunes involved in the wagers, owners and riders resorted to a variety of tricks to ensure success. Eventually the necessity for rules and a body to enforce them became apparent. By the middle of the eighteenth century the Jockey Club had come into existence and its members met regularly at Richard Vernon's coffee house in the High Street.

Elegant society also resorted to Ipswich. Indeed, the town seems to have made a very agreeable impression on visitors. Evelyn recorded:

> The trade of Ipswich is for the most part Newcastle coals which they supply London with; but was formerly clothing. There is not any beggar does ask any alms in the whole town, a thing very extraordinary, so ordered by the prudence of the magistrates. It has in it 14 or 15 very beautiful churches. In a word 'tis for building, cleaness and good order, one of the sweetest towns in England.

And Defoe discovered:

> There is a great deal of very good company in this town and though there are not so many of the gentry here as at Bury, yet there are more here than in any other town in the county: the company you meet with are generally persons well-informed on the world and who have something very solid and entertaining in their society. This may happen by their having a remnant of gentlemen and masters of ships among them who have seen more of the world than the people of an inland town are likely to have seen.

Defoe regarded Ipswich as 'one of the most agreeable places in England' but the reasons he gives for his opinion suggest that the town was more popular with people of modest means than the country gentry: 'good houses at very easy rent . . . a wonderful plenty of all manner of provisions, whether flesh of fowl and very good of its kind . . . so cheap that a family in Ipswich may live better than in any town in England of its bigness . . .

easy passage to London, the coach going through daily'.

Smaller towns also had their attractions for the visitor. Bungay in Defoe's day was enjoying brief fame as a spa. Mr King, a local apothecary, drew attention to the healing properties of the chalybeate spring in the castle. He built a bathhouse and surrounded it with pleasant gardens. The resort proved popular among the Suffolk and Norfolk gentry but its fame never spread further afield and Bungay was unable to outbid its great rival, Bath, for the support of fashionable society. Woodbridge gave an outward appearance of prosperity with its bustling wharfs and warehouses and the shops of prosperous corn and butter merchants. The town had a reputation for producing the best butter in England. 'I have known', says Defoe, 'a firkin of Suffolk butter sent to the West Indies and brought back to England again, and has been perfectly good and sweet, as at first.' In the early eighteenth century there were still signs of the ancient prosperity based on cloth. Long Melford 'is full of very good houses, and, as they told me, is richer and has more wealthy masters of the manufacture in it than in Sudbury'.

The spate of fashionable building of country houses, town houses and facades gave impetus to a well-established local industry. There were important brickfields at Ipswich, Woodbridge, Woolpit, Aldeburgh, Beccles and numerous other small establishments. Eighteenth-century readers of the *Ipswich Journal* were confronted with many advertisements such as this:

> To be sold. At William Robinson's Brick-Kiln in St. Helen's Parish, Ipswich. Pots for Cure of Smoking Chimneys adapted for 9 to 12 and 14-inch Funnels, as good as any in London; also fine Rubbing Bricks and black Cornice, red Pantiles and glazed ditto, and all sorts of Bricks and Tyles. N.B. Gentlemen or Builders may have bricks in any form by sending a Mould.

Restrictions had been placed on the use of timber for building since Elizabethan times, when the needs of the navy had prior claim on the dwindling stocks of oak. By the late seventeenth century genteel society was turning up its nose at timber-framed buildings. When Lady Fiennes visited Bury in the 1690s she sweepingly condemned all its houses and public buildings, except Cupola House, as old-fashioned and rambling. Classical styles demanded the elegance, symmetry and precision which could only be achieved by brick and stone. Suffolk has no stone so ingenious kiln owners overcame the problem by producing the famous 'Suffolk whites' which rapidly superseded red bricks for all-important building. But not all wealthy patrons admired this technical achievement. When the Earl of Bristol was urged by his daughter to use Suffolk whites for his new mansion he replied:

> You beg me on your knees that Ickworth may be built of white stone bricks . . . What! Child, build my house of a brick that looks like a sick, pale, *jaundiced* red brick, that would be red if it could!

Whatever the Earl-Bishop might say, the brickfields were kept busy providing material for the elegant Georgian streets of Ipswich, Melford and Bungay, the splendid Assembly Rooms at Bury, the new mansions such as Heveningham Hall and Shrubland Hall.

It was all very grand. But there was, of course, another Suffolk. In Sudbury, Defoe found 'the number of the poor is almost ready to eat up the rich'. The new draperies manufacturers had been severely hit by the East India Company's trade in cheap silks and calicoes. The clothiers tried various tactics to combat this assault on their livelihood: they petitioned the government to restrict textile imports; they tightened up their guild regulations; they extended their activities to cover silk weaving and enticed craftsmen away from the London silk centre of Spitalfields; they diversified their own industry and produced, among other things, crapes and bunting. It was of little avail. Yorkshire's woollen industry was better equipped to cope with a declining and changing market. It was the mill owners of Lancashire who began to produce the cottons and linens the British people wanted. Slowly the North of England was taking over as the country's industrial centre and would be well poised

113

to benefit from the vastly increased markets opened up by the great imperial drive.

Nor was it only the textile industry which fell on hard times. The fishing ports had lost their battle against the sea. In 1652 the inhabitants of Walberswick appealed to the government for aid for

> our poor town of Walberswick, now one of the poorest towns in England, not being able to repair our church or meeting-place, which at the first was reared up by the inhabitants at their only cost and charge, and the many poor widows and fatherless and motherless children and at this present not above one man living in the town that has £5 per year of his own.

Forty-three years later they unroofed most of their decaying church and used the materials to repair the south aisle, tower and the porch, which was all they used from then on. They were not the first parishioners to do so; Covehithe's magnificent fifteenth-century church was dismantled in 1672. Dunwich, Blythborough, Southwold and, to a lesser extent, Lowestoft shared the same fate as their harbours either disappeared or became too unreliable for regular use by the fishing fleets. In 1670 Suffolk had only 59 fishing boats and the King personally supported a company set up to restore the east coast fisheries. It was only the first of several such ventures which, despite the injection of large amounts of capital, failed.

It is not surprising that more and more fishermen turned to less reputable methods of earning a living. Smuggling became a regular and highly organized industry in this period. When the Commonwealth government and its successors slapped heavy taxes and duties on a variety of commodities they threw down a gauntlet to mariners, foreign traders and English consumers who refused to be balked by such restrictions. Large smuggling associations developed with headquarters in Dunkirk, Flushing, Ostend and Calais. They ran cargoes across to the coves and small harbours of Kent, Essex and Suffolk, often preferring the latter because they were farther from London. Local marin-

ers went out in their small boats to collect cargoes from the 100-
and 200-ton ships which anchored offshore under cover of
darkness, then carried the casks and chests of tea, tobacco and
spirits to regular hiding places where they awaited distribution.
Illicit goods were bestowed under the altar at Theberton
church, beneath the floorboards of Leiston's Nonconformist
meeting house and behind the pulpit at Rishangles (sometimes
during the sermon).

The runs were made with as much regularity as legitimate
trading ventures and, with the majority of the local community
from the squire and parson downwards supporting the
smugglers, the understaffed revenue service had little chance of
catching the criminals. Farmhands could earn 25 shillings a
night plus perks for helping to move contraband. Others were
similarly rewarded for running an information and signalling
service for the benefit of the smuggler. Millers would set their
mill sails in certain ways to let the 'gentlemen' know whether or
not the coast was clear. The owner of Cat House overlooking
the Orwell estuary displayed a large stuffed white cat or
showed a light in an upper window to tell the smugglers they
could come ashore. There was nothing romantic about this
trade and there were many bloody affrays between the
smugglers and the preventive men but the trade would scarcely
have existed at all if it had not been for the harsh economic conditions of the time. It provided not only 'brandy for the parson,
baccy for the clerk'; it provided a living for many families which
would otherwise have starved.

Ipswich shared the decline of the coast towns. Defoe was
dismayed at the sight of the almost idle dockyards: 'why . . . is
Ipswich not capable of building and receiving the greatest ships
in the navy, seeing they may be built and brought up again
within a mile and a half of the town?' The answer was obviously
the growth of London 'which sucks the vitals of trade in this
island to itself'. But Ipswich craftsmen were still building ships,
mainly colliers for the Newcastle–London trade, and were
proud of their high standards. It was their boast that an
Ipswich vessel was good for 50 years or more of regular service.

Throughout the county poverty was the largest single problem. Beyond the growing number of unemployed and unemployable were the mass of those whose earnings were totally inadequate to keep body and soul together. Agricultural labourers were employed on a daily basis at 5*d*. or 6*d*. a day. In the slack seasons of the year, when the weather was bad and when the harvests failed, they had nothing to do but skulk at home or beg in the streets of the nearby town. The yarn industry was flourishing and employed about 36,000 women and children. However the spinsters were paid only 3*d*. or 4*d*. for a full day's work and had to look to the parish for additional help.

Though the poor rate increased in every community, the Elizabethan poor law was quite inadequate in meeting the needs of the depressed rural community. The system had to be supplemented by private acts of charity and many members of the more favoured classes considered such acts as part of their Christian and social responsibility. Gentlemen, merchants, parsons and ladies of noble family founded almshouses, hospitals and schools. They left land and capital sums to provide income for the perpetual relief of the poor. It was not enough. By the middle of the eighteenth century several parishes were seeking from Parliament, 'power of incorporating themselves and of regulating the employment and maintenance of the poor by certain rules not authorized by existing poor laws'. Beginning in 1756 the Acts were passed which gave parishes the authority to acquire funds for the building of 'houses of industry'. Thus came into existence the workhouse, whose chequered history we must follow in our next chapter.

There were, of course, many degrees in society between the merchant or the well-to-do farmer and the casual labourer. The following figures of wages which pertained in the 1680s give some idea of the standing and relative prosperity of semi-skilled workers:

A head gardener	£12 p.a.
A bailiff	£6 p.a.
A reed cutter	1*s*. 5*d*. per day

In 1752 a carpenter could command 1*s*. 10*d*. and a bricklayer (plus his mate) 3*s*. 4*d*. for a day's work. The impermanent nature of many rural occupations is apparent. Parents who wanted a greater degree of security for their children tried to place them 'in service'. Any family aspiring to some social station kept servants and could afford to do so because wages were extremely low. The servants, for their part, accepted their pittance, the long hours, the lack of freedom and the insults of their betters because it would not have occurred to them to do otherwise and because they were reasonably fed, cleanly clothed and, by comparison with the pestilential hovels from which they came, luxuriously accommodated. When Thomas Camborne, Rector of Drinkstone (near Bury) died in 1694 he left land and houses, the rent from which was to go towards the upkeep of the parish poor. Part of this income was laid out in tools for boys and aprons for girls so that they could enter 'service'.

The majority of Suffolk men and women were, of course, employed in agriculture. Throughout most of the period emphasis was still on animal husbandry. Although the dwindling demand for wool slowly reduced the sheep flocks, these beasts still had other uses. Suffolk was a prime supplier of mutton to the London market as well as beef and fowls. Defoe conjures up an intriguing picture of an eighteenth-century 'turkey drive'; 'an inhabitant of the place has counted 300 droves pass in one season over Stratford Bridge on the River Stour; these droves contain from 300 to 1,000 in each drove, so one may suppose them to contain 500 one within the other, which is 150,000 in all'. Dairying was also important. Although Defoe did not like it, Suffolk cheese had a reputation as impressive as Suffolk butter.

One reason why so much acreage was devoted to stock farming was that under the old rotation system, land had to be left fallow every second or third year. Richard Weston's *Discourse Upon Husbandry* had introduced the idea of four-crop rotation in the mid-seventeenth century and Suffolk farmers were the first to put the scheme into operation extensively. By the end of the century many gentleman and yeoman farmers were alternating turnips and clover with their wheat and barley crops. In other parts of the county agricultural improvement was studied almost exclusively on the large estates of the major landowners. Not so in Suffolk. The greatest writer on rural matters (though he was a Suffolk man and may have been biased) observed:

> the most interesting circumstance is . . . the rich yeomanry as they were once called being numerous, farmers occupying their own lands of a value rising £100 to £400 a year: a most valuable set of men who having the means and the most powerful inducements to good husbandry carry agriculture to a high degree of perfection.

By 1760 the Agricultural Revolution was just around the corner. Suffolk, at least, did not come upon it unawares.

Not all Suffolkers lived and died in their native fields. Some young men sought adventure and escape from grinding poverty in the army or the navy. This period saw the formation of Suffolk's own regiment. In June 1685 Henry Howard, Duke of Norfolk, was commissioned by the new King, James II, to raise a regiment of Foot. However, the new unit was of no use to James in his hour of trial. Protestant East Anglia declared for William of Orange in 1688 and its regiment, now under the command of Henry Wharton, fought against the ex-king in Ireland and served with distinction at the Battle of the Boyne. The East Anglian lads went on to fight King William's wars against King Louis in France and the Low Countries. In 1714 the regiment was designated the 12th Regiment of Foot. The Hanoverian kings' German commitments drew England into a succession of continental conflicts and Suffolk's regiments were involved in many of the decisive campaigns. The Twelfth fought under George II at Dettingen (1743), the last occasion on which an English king led his forces into battle. The regiment fought at Fontenoy and at Minden, one of the most remarkable battles fought on European soil. A British contingent of 7,000 men found itself suddenly face to face with the main French army of 10,000 cavalry and 30,000 infantry. With incredible courage and discipline the British force held firm. Not only that; they won the day, accounting for over 7,000 of the enemy. But of the Twelfth's 600 men, half did not return from Minden. Not until 1782 was the Twelfth renamed in honour of the area which had always provided the bulk of its recruits, the East Suffolk Regiment (it became the Suffolk Regiment a century later).

Suffolk men who served in the Royal Navy found themselves engaged in some battles very much nearer home. The Dutch wars brought enemy ships to the coast for the first time since the Viking era. The new danger led to a flurry of activity in Ipswich. The town provided 32 armed merchantmen for the navy, and royal officials descended on the wharfs to set up victualling and supply offices. More sinister were the press gangs who scoured the towns, villages and farms of East Suffolk in search of 'cannon fodder'.

On Saturday 3 June 1665 workers were out in the fields early – before dawn – for the weather was incredibly hot and they wanted to take advantage of the morning coolness. Suddenly they paused in their hoeing as a crash like none-too-distant thunder reverberated around a cloudless sky. It was gunfire and it was coming from a point some 14 miles N.N.E. of Lowestoft. 'The two most mighty and best appointed fleets which any age had ever seen, disputed the command of the greater half of the globe, the commerce of nations and the riches of the universe!' All day long the guns roared and the sound carried across Suffolk and Essex to the capital itself. Along the coast, men and women strained their eyes or plied telescopes seawards but could see nothing except columns of smoke above the horizon. Then, in late afternoon, there came the sound of a mighty explosion that seemed as if it must split the very ocean in twain. Only next day when frigates returning from the battle to unload 2,000 prisoners and 300 sick and wounded at Southwold brought the details, did the eager Suffolkers learn of the destruction of the Dutch flagship, *De Eendracht*, and the complete rout of the enemy. Most of the coast towns had to share the burden of caring for the wounded and prisoners in makeshift hospitals and camps, Southwold receiving as much as £5,900 and Ipswich £8,500 for their services.

The following years saw many alarms and anxieties in the county. There were frequent rumours of Dutch invasion and as frequent appeals from the coast towns for guns and fortifications. Repeated calls were made upon Suffolk to provide men and ships and, in 1667, 26 small vessels were impressed as fire ships by the navy. The county militia had to be kept in a constant state of readiness. The feared 'invasion' took place on 2 July 1667. The Dutch made a combined naval and military assault on Landguard Fort with the object of capturing the new dockyard at Harwich. Fortunately the naval part of the expedition was balked by English intervention but the small Landguard garrison still had to face a determined attack by 1,400 Dutchmen who landed at Felixstowe and advanced along the beach. The Englishmen kept up a daunting musket barrage and after several hours the assailants retreated in confusion. Having now missed the tide the demoralized and hungry soldiers suffered the final indignity of having to wait half the night in shivering groups on the sand, until they could refloat their boats.

Five years later another great naval battle was fought off Suffolk and this time spectators could follow its course. In mid-May 1672 the Anglo-French fleet under the command of the Duke of York and the Earl of Sandwich followed 88 Dutch ships up the Channel. They made the disastrous mistake of putting in at Sole Bay for careening. At dawn on 28 May they were surprised by the enemy. The allies were caught with their sails furled and many of their men sleeping in Southwold's alehouses. With a haste akin to panic the home fleet weighed anchor and tried to manoeuvre away from the lee shore but not before the Dutch had opened fire.

Aroused by the noise, the local inhabitants rushed out on to Gunhill Cliff and Easton Cliffs and from these vantage points they saw it all: the English bearing northwards in ragged order; the French trying to evade the battle; the Dutch raking their opponents with devastating fire – everything was clearly visible on the sunlit sea. The enemy concentrated their fire on the

Prince and the *Royal James* which carried the English admiral and vice-admiral. Sandwich's *Royal James* had much the worse of the battle. Mastless and with half her company dead, she was encircled by enemy men-o'-war and baited by fire ships. At one point it seemed that she might be relieved by Sir Joseph Jordan's squadron but Jordan sailed past her to go to the aid of the Duke of York, conduct which enraged one onlooker:

> I like not his fighting nor conduct, I wished myself on him to have saved that brave Montague [Lord Sandwich], for he was in the wind of him and might have come down to him . . . I was so near as I saw almost every broadside and was in hearing and whistling of the shot.

It was about midday that a Dutch fireship got fatally close to the *Royal James*. The flames reached her magazine and she disintegrated with a sickening roar. Two weeks later, Lord Sandwich's body was picked up by a local ketch. Bloated and scarred, it still proudly carried the George and Star of the Garter on its breast. The Earl was conveyed to Landguard Fort where he lay for a week before being taken to London for a magnificent funeral.

Such excitements were rare interruptions of the more leisurely drama of the passing seasons and the little tragicomedies acted out in Suffolk's halls and hovels, inns and assembly rooms, churches and chapels. Religion continued to be an important issue for many years after the Restoration. The Commonwealth had given rise to a plethora of left wing sects. They ranged from the more orthodox Independents, Presbyterians, Congregationalists and Baptists, who differed mainly from Anglicans in their rejection of episcopacy and ceremonial, to such wilder groups as Quakers (often quite violent in their opposition to the established church and very different to the peaceable folk of later years), Brownists and Fifth Monarchy Men. Harsh laws were passed against all Dissenters at the Restoration and were rigidly enforced (with brief interludes) until 1689. Ministers were ejected from their livings. Nonconformist groups had to meet in secret. Preachers who would not be silent or stay at home were thrown into prison.

Persecution, of course, did not stop the Dissenters and when toleration became the official policy of William and Mary's government, new chapels sprang up all over the county. Nowhere was the Nonconformist movement stronger than in Suffolk. The elegant places of worship they built are continuing proof of their devotion, vigour and wealth. Bury and Ipswich both have fine Unitarian (originally Presbyterian) chapels; Needham Market's Congregational chapel is elegant and Walpole's, the oldest in the county, intimate and charming. It comes as no surprise to learn that when Defoe visited Southwold he attended divine service in the church with 27 local people. When he walked past the dissenting chapel afterwards, he found it full to the doors.

7. PEN, PAINT AND PROGRESS

The Suffolk chronicler is fortunate when he comes to the period of the Industrial and Agrarian Revolutions: he can view the life of the county through the eyes of a glorious company of sensitive observers – Crabbe, Constable, Bloomfield, Gainsborough, Smythe, Fitzgerald, Churchyard. These men take us to the heart of the matter. Whether their subject is the country or the people who inhabit it they show us what Suffolk was like in a way that cold social statistics can never do. Let us, then, survey the life of Suffolk between 1760 and 1880 with these invaluable guides in our company.

The Industrial Revolution proper passed East Anglia by. The growth of the manufacturing North only confirmed an existing trend. The roads, railways and canals which linked the capital with the new centres of industry sucked skill and commerce away from Suffolk's textile towns and ports, and left a residuum of unemployment, despair and drunkenness. Every town and village had its scenes of seeping poverty and squalor. George Crabbe's home town of Aldeburgh was no exception:

Between the roadway and the walls, offence
Invades all eyes and strikes on every sense:
There lie obscure at every open door
Heaps from the earth and sweepings from the floor,

123

> And day by day the mingled masses grow
> As sinks are disembogued and kennels flow.
> There hungry dogs from hungry children steal,
> There pigs and chickens quarrel for a meal:
> There dropsied infants wail without redress
> And all is want and woe and wretchedness.

In this decayed port, warehouses, empty of merchandise, were let out as temporary havens to the homeless and vagabonds. Amidst the dust and rotting timbers men and boys played desultory games

> While gin and snuff their female neighbours share
> And the black beverage in the fractured ware.

The magistrates – representatives of the gentry, wealthier farmers and prosperous tradesmen – were very concerned about the situation. They wanted to alleviate this suffering and they wanted, perhaps more, to avoid the situation in France where a depressed peasantry had risen against their superiors in bloody revolution. But they were always concerned lest the provision of relief should encourage the indolence of what they called the 'undeserving poor' (i.e. those who had no desire to work, as opposed to the 'deserving poor' whose predicament was not of their own making). Their solution was the workhouse.

We can see some of these oppressive buildings still. At One-house the monolithic workhouse by its very size and starkness illustrates with hideous perfection the problem it was built to solve. It did not provide a solution. Within its walls men, women and children found shelter, meagre provision for their needs and hours of backbreaking labour. They did not find their lost self respect. Crabbe was all too familiar with the heartbreaking scenes in the house of industry:

> There children dwell, who know no parents' care;
> Parents, who know no children's love, dwell there!
> Heartbroken matrons on their joyless bed,
> Forsaken wives, and mothers never wed;
> Dejected widows with unheeded tears;

And crippled age with more than childhood fears;
The lame, the blind, and, far the happiest they!
The moping idiot and the madman gay.
Here too the sick their final doom receive,
Here brought, amid the scenes of grief, to grieve . . .
Here sorrowing they each kindred sorrow scan,
And the cold charities of man to man.'

War provided a partial easing of the problem. From 1793 to 1815 England was almost continuously engaged with France in the Revolutionary and Napoleonic Wars. Men were pressed into the army and navy. Some were never to see their native fields again; some were to return broken and useless – lifelong charges upon 'the parish'. Fate evened out the poverty statistics. As the years of tumult succeeded one another with little prospect of decisive victory or peace the need for men in the armed forces became acute. The war was a hard time on the coastal community. The press gangs were very active. No ships in harbour could be manned until the navy's requirements had been met and even fishermen – usually exempt – were impressed. Still there were not enough sailors for the ships of Nelson and Collingwood, and regular levies were made on the counties, Suffolk being asked for about 300 men a year.

As Napoleon's power grew prodigiously, the threat of invasion became very real. Home defence was a matter of urgency and the regular forces had to be supplemented by volunteer reserves. A force of Yeomanry known as the Suffolk Light Dragoons was raised at Bury and a part time navy, the Sea Fencibles, patrolled the coast. These bodies of amateur soldiers and sailors were very unreliable and many men joined them to evade conscription to the real army and navy. As an additional deterrent to French invasion the south and east coasts were studded with Martello Towers, small fortresses on which cannons were mounted. Eighteen were raised along the Suffolk shoreline. Whether or not they gave the local people much sense of security we cannot now tell.

The war was a good time for Suffolk farmers. Napoleon's

continental blockade, though never successful, matched the British government's conviction that 'by agriculture alone we live in plenty without intercourse with other nations'. There were also hungry soldiers and sailors as well as beleaguered allies to feed. The accent was therefore on intensive farming. The exigencies of war thus gave an added boost to the Agrarian Revolution which had already begun.

Scientific stock breeding, sophisticated systems of crop rotation, use of fertilizers, reclamation of waste land, regional specialization – all these were marks of the new approach to farming. Suffolk gave the world three great breeds of domestic animals during this period – the Black Face sheep, the Red Poll and the Suffolk Punch. The great pioneers of the mid-eighteenth century, like Robert Bakewell, had shown not only that attention to diet – and, in particular, the use of root crops for winter feed – produced bigger, healthier animals but also that it was possible, by in-breeding, to achieve in animals just those characteristics which are required. Wool was now of little importance to sheep farmers in Suffolk. What they wanted were ewes which produced a large number of lambs, with a high meat quality. Many Suffolk farmers were experimenting in the early 1800s and gradually it became clear that the best results were obtained by crossing Norfolk horned ewes (whose traditional qualities were fecundity and hardiness) with Southdown rams (famed for their fattening qualities). Known first of all as 'Black-faces', they were eventually classified as a distinct breed – Suffolk Sheep. The Earl of Stradbroke was among the early enthusiastic champions of the breed and his famous shepherd Ishmael Cutter produced some remarkable results on the Earl's pastures near Eye. In 1837 he raised 606 lambs from 413 ewes, a considerable achievement in the days before artificial feedstuffs.

Dairying, as we have seen, had long been an important feature of Suffolk rural life. The butter produced here, as Kirby's *Suffolk Traveller* affirmed in 1734, was 'justly esteemed the pleasantest and best in England'. Most of the milk that went into Suffolk butter and cheese came from the old Suffolk dun cow. Various breeding experiments were made during the first half of the next century but it was eventually discovered that the traditional breed could not be improved on for milk yield and early maturity. From then on farmers concentrated on developing the latent potential of what came to be called the Red Poll, and foremost among breeders were the Biddels of Playford.

Most famous and best loved of all the shire horses is the Suffolk Punch. The founding sire from whom all these noble animals descend was owned by Thomas Crisp of Ufford in the 1760s. In 1784 Sir John Cullum described the qualities of the breed in his *History of Hawstead*:

> They are not made to indulge the rapid impatience of this posting generation; but for draught, they are perhaps unrivalled, as for their gentle and tractable temper; and to exhibit proofs of their great power, drawing matches are sometimes made and the proprietors are as anxious for the success of their respective horses, as those can be whose racers aspire to the plates at Newmarket.

The great pioneer names in agriculture – Coke of Holkham, Jethro Tull, Robert Bakewell – belong to other counties. Nevertheless Suffolk's claim to leadership in the Agrarian Revolution is unassailable. Early widespread interest in breeding, crop rotation, ploughing matches, and so on led to the informal meetings of farmers to discuss their common problems. From this grew the nationwide organization of Farmers Clubs, of which the Ashbocking Club, founded in 1837, was the first. Six years before that the East Suffolk Association, forerunner of the Suffolk Agricultural Association, was formed. In 1832 it staged the first county show at Wickham Market, a modest event at which, in the words of the *Ipswich Journal* 'the exhibition of stock was anything but great, yet what was shown was of superior quality'. From this simple beginning was to develop the modern, vast two-day show, one of the most popular annual events in East Anglia.

Suffolk also produced the man who more than any other may be called 'the evangelist of the Agrarian Revolution'. Communications were primitive in Georgian and early Victorian

England and the spread of ideas depended largely on propagandists who wrote books, published journals and addressed meetings. Arthur Young devoted most of his life to these activities. He was born in 1741, son of the rector of Bradfield Combust, inherited farmland in the parish and tried to work it – with disastrous results. He fared no better when he transferred his agricultural activities to Essex and later Hertfordshire. But though he lacked the resources and, perhaps, the application to put his ideas into successful practice, he had ideas in plenty about farming. In 1768 he published *A Six Weeks' Tour Through the Southern Counties of England and Wales*, the first of many books and pamphlets in which he surveyed the current state of agriculture in the regions of Britain. In 1784 he began a monthly journal, *Annals of Agriculture*, which covered every aspect of the subject and ran for a quarter of a century. By 1793 he was recognized as one of the foremost authorities on farming and was appointed secretary to the newly formed Board of Agriculture. The following year his *General View of the Agriculture of the County of Suffolk* appeared – only one of a veritable torrent of works flowing from his pen. Young gave wide publicity to every new idea. He advocated enclosure, reclamation and the establishment of large farming units on which the latest innovations could be economically employed. In a word, he advocated greater professionalism in farming.

It was this professionalism that lay at the root of those changes in agriculture of which Suffolk folk were most readily aware. Edward Fitzgerald, the Woodbridge poet and eccentric, was certainly alive to them. 'The county about here', he wrote, 'is the cemetary of so many of my oldest friends; and the petty race of squires who have succeeded only use the earth for an investment . . . So I get to the water, where friends are not buried nor pathways stopped up.' Encouraged by the government and directly patronized by George III ('Farmer George'), farming became fashionable. Landowners great and small built themselves splendid new houses at the centres of their estates; they went shooting and hunting together (The Duke of Grafton hunted hounds here from 1745 until the early nineteenth century. The Waveney Harriers were formed about the same time. The Suffolk Hunt was established by George Mure of Herringswell in 1823). Their ladies played the harpsichord and the new forte-piano, paid visits to each other, organized balls and made up theatre parties. The county's major towns were revived as provincial centres of fashion, aping the customs of the capital. William Cobbett in his *Rides* was so impressed by Bury St Edmunds with its thronged Assembly Rooms, newly-opened Theatre Royal and Botanical Gardens, and its elegant sedan chair and carriage-borne upper class that he called it 'the nicest town in the world'.

But far more evocative than words of the life of Suffolk's gentlemen farmers are the paintings of Thomas Gainsborough. The great artist found fame and spent most of his life in London but he learned his love of landscape in the countryside round his native Sudbury where, as a lad, he wandered the fields and lanes, sketchbook in hand. He moved to Ipswich in 1750 and soon found that while no-one wanted to buy 'landskips' the provincial élite clamoured for portraits which would immortalize their own concept of themselves – lords of their own little bits of creation. Gainsborough obliged, and grasped the opportunity to combine portraits with pictures of his own beloved Suffolk. His paintings were of beautiful sweeps of sunlit country inhabited by beautiful people. They were idealized scenes in which it was always summer, the corn ever ripe, the feathery-leafed trees always casting a delicious shade and his sitters' langorous fingers and satin shoes never coming in contact with rural mud. Even Gainsborough's peasants – for he sometimes painted country scenes for his own pleasure – were figures of heroic simplicity for whom life was a merry frolic in the warm harvest fields.

For the men and women who could live in the heart of the rural community and yet be so far shielded from reality as to indulge such fantasies, life was, indeed, good. Over many years large-scale farming in Suffolk paid well – especially cereal farming. The French wars coincided with a run of bad harvests (14 poor harvests and 2 good ones in 22 years). Since the disruption of trade prevented foreign corn reaching English shores, the price of home-grown grain rocketed. Farmers hurried to profit from this situation, and the heavy claylands of central Suffolk came into their own. It was then that the Suffolk landscape took on its now familiar appearance – the heaths and meadows of east and west harbouring fat flocks and herds, the centre dominated by wide fields, interrupted by occasional copses and water-meadows. When the war ended the special conditions which had favoured this prosperity ended with it. In 1815 corn prices plummetted to half what they had been in the peak year of 1812. Parliament, where the landed interest was dominant, hastened to pass the Corn Law which prohibited the import of foreign grain until the price had reached 80s. a quarter. For 31 years this appalling piece of legislation remained on the statute book, protecting farm profits at the expense of every man, woman and child in the country, who had to pay inflated prices for daily bread.

The situation would not have been so bad if all sections of the rural community had shared the benefits brought by protection. They did not. Because there were more potential workers than jobs, wages remained low. Rationalization meant that farmers kept their permanent staffs to a minimum and drew on the large pool of casual labour at the busy seasons of the year. Most workers lived in thatched, verminous medieval cottages or in farmhouses, made redundant by the amalgamation of farms, converted into smaller units by flimsy partitions, steep stairs and lean-to additions. Some farmers built new dwellings for their workers. While many of them were minute and substandard, others were responsibly built, and from 1838 the Royal Agricultural Society addressed itself vigorously to the problem. Those erected by Lord Tollemache on his estate at Helmingham are an excellent example of the best in modest domestic architecture. Properly built houses were excellent but the farmworker's basic need was for food. Like everyone else, he had to buy bread at artificially inflated prices and he needed higher wages in order to do so. This is precisely where the prevailing poor law worked to his disadvantage and in his employer's favour. The Speenhamland System, which operated from 1795 to 1834, provided that where a labourer's wage was inadequate (and this was calculated with reference to the current price of bread) it could be augmented from the poor rate. This demoralized farm workers by bringing them within the category of the parish poor; it deprived them of any incentive to work; it subsidized the farmers by relieving them of the obligation to pay realistic wages. The depressed labourers did not always suffer in silence. Organized despair showed itself in widespread support for the Chartist movement of the 1830s and in sporadic outbursts of rick-burning. Between 1835 and 1837, a period of particular hardship, the steady trickle of people leaving the county became a flood, after the Poor Law Amendment Act provided for financial assistance for those wishing to emigrate. Of the 6,403 people who took advantage of the scheme, 1083 were from Suffolk; most of them emigrated to Canada. At the same time more than 2,000 left home to try their fortunes in the industrial North.

It is a depressing enough picture but the life of the rural peasant was not one of unrelieved misery and squalor. For anyone with eyes to see, living in the Suffolk countryside had its compensations. Such a one was Robert Bloomfield of Honington (1766–1823). As a child he lived with his mother who gained a meagre living from her dame school. He became a farm worker at Sapiston at the age of eleven and kept it up until it broke his health. He went to London and found eventual success there in the literary world of Wordsworth and Coleridge who admired the freshness and authenticity of his nature poetry. Fame and fortune proving, alike, fickle, Bloomfield died, poor and half-blind in Bedfordshire.

The inspiration for his best work (and *The Farmer's Boy* is the greatest) came from his years of hard and varied labour at Sapiston. There is little hint of bitterness or self-pity in his verses; Bloomfield exulted in the country life:

> Fresh from the Hall of Bounty sprung
> With glowing heart and ardent eye,
> With songs and rhyme upon my tongue,

131

And fairy visions dancing by,
The mid-day sun in all his power,
The backward valley painted gay;
Mine was the road without a flower,
Where one small streamlet crossed the way.

In *The Farmer's Boy* the poet traces the career of his simple hero, Giles, through the four seasons of the farming year. It is an everyday saga and one which recreates for us with freshness and vigour the rural life of two centuries ago.

Where woods and groves in solemn grandeur rise,
Where the kite brooding unmolested flies,
The woodcock and the painted pheasant race
And skulking foxes destined for the chase;
There GILES, untaught and unrepining stray'd
Through every copse and grove and winding glade;
There his first thought to Nature's charm inclined,
That stamps devotion on th'enquiring mind.

We find the same attitude of honest delight in Suffolk's greatest creative genius. John Constable (1776–1837) also loved his home country, spent most of his life away from it and was always striving to recapture its moods in his work. 'I have been running after pictures and seeking truth at second hand,' he wrote to a friend. 'I shall return to Bergholt, where I shall endeavour to get a pure and unaffected manner of representing the scenes that may employ me . . . The great vice of the present day is *bravura*, an attempt to do something beyond the truth. Fashion always had and always will have its day, but truth in all things only will last, and can only have just claims on posterity.' So Constable returned to his beloved Dedham Vale, the country he learned so intimately when he was growing up midst the rumble and roar of his father's mill wheels. And he made those pictures which have always been recognized as representing not just Suffolk but essential England.

It was an England which was soon to change; perhaps that is why Constable's paintings evoke such a nostalgic response in all of us. The most obvious change was the coming of the railway. Before Constable died, plans were afoot which would carry steam trains across the Stour estuary and up to Ipswich within sound of East Bergholt. In 1836 the Eastern Counties Railway Co. was formed to build and operate a line from London to Yarmouth via Colchester, Ipswich and Norwich (i.e. it was to be in direct competition with the coach services which followed the same route). These were the early days of the railway mania and the E.C.R.Co's project was the most ambitious to date. It was too ambitious; when it reached Colchester in 1843 work stopped because local shareholders were outbidded by others who were all for getting the stock (and profits) rolling and had lost interest in meeting the transport needs of Suffolk and Norfolk. As the *Norwich Mercury* bitterly remarked local people might have ensured the line by buying up shares 'for a sum not larger than was expended in bribery at the last Norwich election'.

But an Ipswich businessman, J. C. Cobbold, formed another company, the Eastern Union, to complete the work. By 1849 Ipswich had been linked to Bury and Norwich, and branch tracks linked Harwich, Hadleigh and Sudbury to the main line. There now began a bitter battle between the two companies. The E.C.R.Co. was worried because the Ipswich–Norwich line was in direct competition with its own Eastern Counties and Norfolk Railway which linked Norwich with the capital via Cambridge. In fact the E.C.R.Co. held the whip hand; they still controlled the line south of Colchester and by fixing high through fares they were able to force the majority of Norwich travellers to use the alternative route. In 1854 the Eastern Union was forced to sell out to its rivals. Other branch lines were laid by small local companies, bringing Lowestoft, Beccles, Halesworth, Framlingham and Woodbridge into the steam age. All these endeavours were eventually gobbled up by the E.C.R.Co. which was reconstituted as the Great Eastern Railway Company in 1862.

Mention of electioneering practices in Norwich brings us to the political history of Georgian and Victorian Suffolk. This period saw considerable changes in the field of domestic politics. The archaic system of representation was at last challenged in the Reform Bill of 1832 and this proved to be the prelude to far-reaching electoral reforms. At the beginning of the nineteenth century Suffolk's parliamentary representation, unaltered for 200 years, was as follows: 2 county members and 2 members each for Ipswich, Bury, Sudbury, Orford, Dunwich, Eye and Aldeburgh. This disposition of the franchise represented a state of affairs which had not existed since medieval times. All the coast towns had dwindled in importance and Dunwich was one of the most notorious rotten boroughs in the country; it consisted of only a handful of houses and its corporation had to exercise their electoral functions in a boat anchored over the centre of the submerged town. Virtually all votes were controlled by local magnates: Bury was a 'pocket borough' of the earls of Bristol, Lord Hereford controlled Orford, Eye's voters submitted to the wishes of Lord Cornwallis, and so on.

Voters who were not tenants of the local landlord or in some other way dependent on him were in a position of power; they could, and usually did, sell their favours to the highest bidder. The normal rate in Ipswich was £3 but this rose steadily as polling time drew nearer and could be as much as £30 on the day. Candidates were expected to give sumptuous banquets for the electors and to give presents to their wives. Bribery was one way of shortening the odds; nobbling the opponent's supporters was another. Corruption and violence were the customary accompaniments of all elections but Sudbury had a particularly notorious reputation. The mayor openly advertised that he and his colleagues were for sale. Bands of burly electioneers wandered the town 'persuading' voters to join their camp and wear their candidate's favours. Once a voter had been recruited he was 'cooped' (i.e. confined) in a local hostelry, there to be plied with beer and kept away from the opposition – unless the opposition chose to invade their rival's stronghold. It is small wonder that Sudbury was the thinly disguised scene of the Eatanswill election which figured so hilariously in Dicken's Pickwick Papers.

The 1832 Reform Bill gave Suffolk 4 county members and

deprived Dunwich, Orford and Aldeburgh of their representation. It also extended the vote by reducing the property qualification. Now, £10 householders in towns and £10 copy holders in the county were enfranchised. But corrupt practices could not be stopped until the secret ballot was introduced (1872). Yet that event held little interest for the majority of Suffolk people. Politics was a game for the rich which held no relevance for them! Even the Reform Act of 1867 which, in deference to pressures from the new industrial centres, gave the vote to urban householders left most members of the rural community unrepresented.

I said at the beginning of this chapter that the Industrial Revolution passed Suffolk by. While Birmingham and Coventry were growing and spreading like grimy stains over the countryside; while new enterprise was ripping open the hills and valleys of Durham and South Wales; while northerners were exchanging fresh air for back-to-back housing and regular wages, the face of Suffolk remained unchanged and her people continued in the traditional ways, most of them never venturing more than a few miles from their own village. But the era of steam and the worshipping of progress had come to stay and not even Suffolk could remain completely unmoved by the spirit of the age. The coming of the railways, the development of agriculture, the multifarious demands of the *noveau riche* class created new industries and revitalized old ones.

The vestiges of the cloth industry were still to be found in the south of the county. A little woollen cloth was still made for local consumption but it was being replaced by such mixed textiles as fustians, hempen cloths and drabbet. The latter, named for its greyish-white colour, was used principally in the making of farmers' smocks. The weaving was still done, in the traditional manner, by craftsmen working at home. They were not organized as a corporate body but were completely in the hands of the entrepreneurs, and were lucky to realize 6s. or 7s. for a hard week's work, which meant that they were worse off than a fully employed farm worker. Yet, the story of the Suffolk weavers is one of the more remarkable in the history of our county.

For 900 years they continued, adapting themselves to changing circumstances, and only in recent years did the last loom fall silent in Lavenham. It was traditional skills and low wages which brought London silk manufacturers to a number of towns and villages between Ipswich and Haverhill in the eighteenth century. In course of time cottage industry was replaced by the factory system. Mills powered by water or steam were built in Hadleigh, Glemsford and Nayland, and at Sudbury many handloom operators and their machines were installed in factories where the employer could exercise more control over them. The fortunes of the industry fluctuated but at its peak it employed as many as 1,500 people in the production of plain and figured silks, satins and velvets.

There was one industry in Suffolk which had been ancient when the first weaver set up his loom. Flint working and knapping probably has a continuous history in the Brandon area from Neolithic times. For many centuries this industry had taken second place to the rearing of sheep on the Breckland heaths. When the woollen cloth industry declined, whatever specialized sheep farming continued in the county despised the meagre pastures of the west. Sporting estates, rabbit farming and limited barley production were all that this area was good for – except flint. It was used steadily for building walls and instead of brick in the humbler farmhouses and cottages. Many of the county's more impressive churches (such as that at Lavenham) and public buildings were dressed with flint. In the nineteenth century there was a revival in the use of flint as a building material for labourers' cottages, railway stations and municipal buildings. At the same time flint was being put to quite a different use. The battle of Waterloo is supposed to have been won on the playing fields of Eton. It might be claimed with equal justification that it was won in the flintyards of Brandon. For thence came the flints used in the firing mechanisms of the English guns which wrought such havoc among the Napoleonic cavalry and infantry. A Brandon flint was reckoned to be good for 500 shots.

The demands of the new agriculture soon proved to be too great for the traditional manufacturers of farm implements –

the blacksmiths and wheelwrights. Progressive farmers wanted traditional tools such as ploughs and hoes of improved design as well as such innovations as mechanical drills and harvesting equipment. Richard Garrett of Leiston started his working life as a blacksmith but his skill as a manufacturer of scythes and sickles won him more than a local reputation and in 1778 he set up a foundry where he employed 50 or more men to manufacture these and other tools. Garrett's business became one of the many to experiment with Jethro Tull's horse-drawn seed drill and to introduce many refinements into what became known as the Suffolk drill.

By the early nineteenth century there were many small firms like Garrett's coping with the demand for agricultural machinery, but the one which was destined to be the most successful and longlasting was Ransome's. Robert Ransome came from a Quaker family of Norwich where he had established a brass and iron foundry. In 1789 he set up in business at the Orwell Works in Ipswich where his skill in wrought and cast iron work extended well beyond the sphere of agricultural machinery. In 1819 Ransome and Sons constructed Ipswich's first iron bridge (Stoke Bridge) and, when the railway was abuilding, they won the contract for supplying the chairs which secured the rails to the sleepers. But the firm's first loyalty was to the farming community. James and Robert, the founder's sons, were among the first members of the Royal Agricultural Society and they won many of the Society's medals for their patented machines.

The Company's single most important innovation came in its early days. To prevent the rapid blunting of plough shares Robert Ransome senior devised, in 1803, a casting process which produced a blade whose under side was harder than its top side. The wearing away of the upper part thus ensured that a keen cutting edge was maintained. Such a development was especially important to the grain farmers of the heavy clay belt. This was only one of numerous patents obtained by Ransomes during its first century and by 1850 the Company was employing over 1,500 men.

Many a visitor wandering the dock area of Ipswich has been

struck by the name 'Coprolite Street' and thought 'There is obviously a story there'. Indeed there is – the story of another Suffolk pioneering endeavour. In 1843 the Rev'd Professor John Henslow was staying with relatives at Felixstowe. Professor Henslow was one of the foremost botanists of his day and was particularly interested in fertilizers. It had recently been discovered that exhausted soil needed nitrogen and phosphates to revive it and the first fertilizer to be applied was Peruvian guano. Henslow noticed that the red cragg and London clay of the neighbourhood contained phosphatic nodules. The Professor's discovery was taken up by Edward Packard, a Saxmundham chemist, who was already producing artificial fertilizer from bones. From the Ransomes he bought an old flour mill on the Ipswich dockside and began the commercial exploitation of the phosphatic nodules which Henslow had called 'coprolites'. Used first by Suffolk farmers, the new fertilizer was soon taken up enthusiastically by foreign agriculturalists, and another commodity was added to Ipswich's regular exports.

The railways, of course, provided welcome labour for large numbers of Suffolk men. There was track to be laid and maintained, there were stations to be built and staffed, and eventually there were train crews to be provided. Even some of the E.C.R. and E.U.R. rolling stock was made locally by the Ipswich firms of Quadling and Turner.

It was the railway which revived the struggling coast towns. None of them better deserved the eventual return of prosperity than Lowestoft. Its inhabitants, and particularly its leading men, were possessed of a local pride, a tenacity of purpose and an ingenuity that few other communities could boast. An excellent example of this is the enterprise begun there in 1757, an enterprise unique in East Anglia.

Hewlin Luson, Esq. of Gunton Hall, near Lowestoft, having discovered some fine clay or earth in that parish, sent a small quantity of it to one of the china manufactories near London with a view of discovering what kind of ware it was capable of producing, which upon trial proved to be finer than that called the Delft ware . . . He immediately procured some workmen from London and erected upon his estate at Gunton a temporary kiln and furnace and all the other apparatus necessary for the undertaking; but the manufacturers in London being apprised of his intentions . . . so far tampered with the workmen he had procured that they spoiled the ware and thereby frustrated Mr Luson's design.'

But Luson was undeterred and within months the Lowestoft porcelain factory was securely established. It flourished until 1803, importing by sea, coal and essential raw materials, and exporting by the same means elegant dishes, tea services, punch bowls and mugs in a variety of vigorous patterns and colours to excite the admiration of fashionable society. Much of the output went to the homes of wealthy East Anglians but there was always a trade to other parts of the kingdom and even to Holland. This is even more remarkable when you think of the strong competition Lowestoft faced from the London and Staffordshire potteries which had definite geographical advantages. It was that competition, however, which eventually forced the factory to close in 1803.

At this time Lowestoft was a 'decayed' town of 2,332 (1801 census) inhabitants. Many efforts were made to improve the port, culminating in the building of the harbour in 1831, but all to no avail. Then, along came Sir Henry Morton Peto. He was one of the more remarkable men thrown up by the Victorian economic boom. In fact, he is the copybook 'self made man' of that era. Inheriting a London building firm, he expanded it rapidly and became involved in many of the important building projects of the day – Nelson's Column, Woolwich Docks, the Houses of Parliament, the Crystal Palace and thousands of miles of railway at home and abroad. He amassed (and later lost) an immense fortune. He entered Parliament and was awarded a baronetcy. In 1844 he bought the estate of Somerleyton with its delightful Tudor house. This he rebuilt, with more vigour than taste. He restored the church and virtually reconstructed the whole village. It was this man who brought a branch of the E.C.R. to Lowestoft in 1847. All at once Lowestoft became the harbour for Norwich and through Norwich was accessible to the rest of the country. The fisheries revived. Lowestoft became an important point of call for coasters. In 1854 the local authorities were empowered by the Lowestoft Improvement Act to levy a 2s. rate to repair buildings, build new homes, instal lighting, sewerage and other amenities. In 1861 the population was 9,413 – and still growing.

By this time other coast towns had begun to share in the revival. Resorts were popular and the railways brought holidaymakers near, if not right into, the east coast towns. In Southwold local businessmen embarked on an ambitious programme of speculative house and hotel building. White's *Directory* for 1844 stated, 'Felixstowe is now in high celebrity as a bathing place, and speculators have within the last few years erected here neat houses and cottages, which are let to visitors during the bathing season'. Aldeborough and Orford became popular with yachtsmen. It was not only the eccentric Edward Fitzgerald ('Old Fritz') who could say, 'I am happiest going in my little boat round the coast to Aldbro', with some bottled porter and some bread and cheese, and some good rough soul who works the boat and chews his tobacco in peace.'

Despite all the changes and the inevitable entry of progress into the county it was the essential Suffolk which captivated the more sensitive inhabitants and visitors. The unique quality of the light, the wide vistas, the rich texture of field, copse and hedgerow, the mellowed cottages, the stately church towers, the mills, the rivers, the shore and the human and animal participants in the landscape – all these attracted the admiration and talents of poets and painters. A century of great artists in the Constable tradition devoted themselves to the Suffolk scene – Thomas Churchyard, the Smythe brothers ('E.R.' and Thomas), John Duvall, Robert Burrows, John Moore and a host of lesser geniuses. They found a deep truth in the simple beauty of the land and, like Constable, they knew that 'truth in all things only will last'.

8. GOOD OLD DAYS AND BAD OLD DAYS

With this chapter we enter the ambit of living memory, the days gilded by nostalgia or tarnished with bitter reminiscence. The chronicler must tread warily to avoid the incorrect detail or unfortunate nuance for which an indignant older citizen may take him to task. During the period 1860–1940 the pace and style of life changed more radically than in any preceding period. Mechanization came to the farms; piped water to the villages; street lighting and trams to the towns. Radio and telephone pierced the isolation of rural areas. Trades unions and unfamiliar political concepts frontally attacked the centuries-old social structure, while the fifth column of economic decline worked from within to weaken its defences. Patronage and paternalism were replaced by 'equality' and the assertion of new rights – education, housing, fair wages. A generation of Suffolk sons was buried on the western front and another generation, in its turn, prepared to fight for a way of life which held little but unemployment, misery and despair for many.

Let us start where most men and women still were – on the land.

Notwithstanding the care, knowledge, and intelligence which are put into the working of the land, under present conditions it can scarcely be made to pay. The machinery works, the mill goes round; the labourers, those who are left of them, earn their wage such as it is, and the beast his provender; the goodman rises early and rest late, taking thought for the day and the morrow, but when at Michaelmas he balances his books there is no return, and lo! The bailiff is glaring through the gates . . . in our parts the ancient industry of agriculture is nearly moribund, and if the land, or the poorer and therefore the more considerable portion of it, is farmed fairly, it is in many instances being worked at a loss, or at any rate without a living profit . . . The small men only too often keep up the game till beggary overtakes them, when they adjourn to the workhouse . . . The larger farmers . . . at last take refuge in a cottage, or, if they are fortunate, find a position as a steward upon some estate. The landlords . . . unless they have private means to draw on . . . sink and sink until they vanish beneath the surface of the great sea of English society.

That depressing picture was painted in 1898 by Henry Ryder Haggard, who could claim to know what he was talking about since he farmed a considerable amount of land on the Suffolk-Norfolk border.

The decline began about 1875. By industry and improved techniques British farmers had survived the ending of protection and had prospered during the middle years of the century. Then the full impact of free trade was felt. Grain from the new American prairie farms was carried to New England ports in new steam trains, exported in new steam ships and sold on the English market at prices lower than home produced corn. In 1877 wheat was 56s.9d. a quarter. By 1894 the price had slumped to 22s.10d. At that figure it could not be grown in England at a profit. By the end of the century the amount of land under cereals in Suffolk had been cut by half. Those farmers who could do so diversified and began rearing stock. But this area was not free from competition: refrigerator ships were bringing cheap lamb and beef from New Zealand and Argentina. A century before, the landed interest had dominated Parliament and had forced the Corn Laws through but the balance of political power had shifted; the middle class and the town dwellers benefited from cheap, imported foodstuffs and so free trade had come to stay.

The depression which fell upon the agrarian community was the worst that it had ever experienced. Land values and rents tumbled. Thousands of labourers were thrown out of work and left their ancestral homes. Ditches and hedges were unkempt, fields unploughed, houses, cottages and barns could not be repaired. Men who had once owned their own farms were now living on the parish dole – a pound of flour and 3*d*. a day. The army of the poor grew daily – a bemused and powerless host who knew not how to relieve their misery. To some the young trade union movement seemed to hold out hope. All over the county workers combined into groups instinctively believing that solidarity meant strength. Just as instinctively farmers felt that solidarity meant trouble. They dismissed or threatened to dismiss any men who held a union card. Usually they won but, in 1874, a sufficient number of labourers stood firm enough to enable an effective strike to be mounted. The demand was for 14*s*. a week. There were violent scenes in many places. In Brandon troops were called in to confront a crowd armed with sticks and bearing a banner proclaiming 'Bread or Blood in Brandon this day'. The demonstrators won on this occasion, the magistrates agreeing to provide cheaper bread and flour, and the triumphant cry of revolt was taken up elsewhere. From Halesworth to Ely the country was up, breaking into shops and barns threatening farmers and magistrates. It was several days before law and order were restored.

Such violence expressed everything and solved nothing. There was no solution: the workers were powerless, the farmers were powerless, even the government was powerless. One farmer complained in a letter to *The Times*,

We have to pay more for labour, manures and feeding stuffs. Yet we are selling the best wheat England ever produced at 25*s*. per quarter, wool has reached the lowest price ever recorded, and, notwithstanding the poor root crop, beef hardly averages 6*d*. per lb. But there is another feature of the farming outlook which is very sad to contemplate, and that is the decreasing influence agriculture has upon Parliament.

Ryder Haggard also felt bitter particularly when he saw good workmen ending their days in the house of correction. He described the workhouse men who worshipped in his church.

> They could not read and I doubt if they understood much of what was passing, but I observed consideration in their eyes. Of what? Of the terror and the marvel of existence, perhaps, and of that good God whereof the parson is talking in those long unmeaning words. God? They know more of the devil and all his works; ill paid labour, poverty, pain, and the infinite, unrecorded tragedies of humble lives. God? They have never found Him. He must live beyond the workhouse wall, out there, in the graveyard, in the waterlogged holes where very shortly . . .

It was a wretched situation and it continued until it was overtaken by an even greater tragedy, the First World War.

There were always people who cared about the fate of their fellows and tried to do something for them. One of the more remarkable – a man well in advance of his time – was the Rev'd Wickham Tozer, Minister of St Nicholas Congregational Church, Ipswich. He decided, in 1884, that there must be a better way of helping the able-bodied poor than doling out daily portions of soup and bread. With the help of other local worthies he founded the Ipswich Labour Bureau. Tozer advertised in the local press, installed a telephone to communicate with local firms and provided clean clothes so that prospective employees could make themselves presentable for interviews. Hundreds of men were registered at the bureau and many of them were found jobs, some as far away as Scotland. For his labours Tozer was misunderstood, even abused, but he persevered with his work and urged other towns and cities to start similar schemes. Yet it was not until 1909 that the government brought in the Labour Exchange Act which led to the setting up of those employment offices which are now so vital a part of the social and industrial scene.

Times may have been hard but the seasonal rhythm of the land had to be maintained. Where modern technology could increase yield or cut overheads without involving prohibitive capital expenditure farmers hurried to utilize it. This was when the agricultural contractor came into his own. He hired to the farmers the large machines and the operators they could not afford to buy for themselves. Most important of all was the steam threshing outfit. This could do in a few days the work which had previously been one of the jobs which kept farm staff occupied throughout the winter. The outfit consisted of a massive steam traction engine, connected by a belt drive to a yet more massive box-like contraption which housed the mechanical beaters, and sticking out from this, like the spout of a tea pot, the elevator which carried away the discarded straw. Steam threshing was a busy, noisy, back-breaking time, as much a highlight of the farming year as harvest itself. Under the eagle eye of the driver (whose machine and team were on piece work) the sweating crew of contracted and farm labour moved quickly about their tasks, trying to keep the pulsating monster fed, empty sacks fitted, and full sacks removed promptly, so that the machine did not have to stop. The thresher's hoppers filled sacks with chaff and with graded grain. A full sack of oats weighed 12 stones, one of barley 16 stones and a sack of wheat was 18 stones, and each one had to be stacked or carted as soon as it was full. Hard work indeed, but warm work on a cold or wet winter's day and the cheerful banter between members of the team helped the time to pass.

Steam machinery was much too heavy for most of the everyday jobs about the farm and the horse continued to provide most of the motive power. Progressive farmers could, however, buy a great variety of machines such as horse-drawn drills, hoes, reapers and binders, which minimized the human element and cut running costs. Ransomes (which became Ransomes, Sims and Jefferies during this period) and Garretts of Leiston were still leaders among firms producing agricultural equipment. They kept abreast of the times and turned out traction engines and steam lorries. But in this industry, too, the writing was on the wall, as Ryder Haggard discovered when he wanted to buy a reaper:

> I have been to Bungay this afternoon to look at a specimen which is highly recommended, a very light but strong and serviceable machine of American make. It is curious, by the way, that the Americans should have won such a hold of the market in agricultural machinery. I suppose that there are English-made reapers . . . I should have been glad to buy one, but there do not seem to be any on show at Bungay.

While lamenting this example of what seems to be a permanent failing in British industry, we must point out that at this very time Ransomes were notching up another important 'first'. As early as 1899 they began to adapt the internal-combustion engine to lawn mowing and in 1902 they patented the first ever ride-on mower.

It was certainly the inventive and thrusting Americans who were to the fore in marketing here that machine which was to bring about a second Agrarian Revolution – the tractor. The first of these vehicles appeared in Suffolk during World War I, a heavy, iron-wheeled machine that looks as though it must frequently have sunk into the soil it was turning.

War once again proved an economic blessing to Suffolk farmers. The government encouraged self-sufficiency by guaranteeing fair prices for cereals and root crops and by establishing a fixed minimum wage for farmworkers. For a brief spell agriculture became a paying proposition and wise farmers salted away their profits in anticipation of a return to hard times.

They were soon vindicated. In 1921 the government repealed the legislation which had protected prices and wages. Cheap foreign produce flooded on to the market and there was a swift return to the dreary pre-war situation – workers laid off and a drastic reduction of land area under cultivation (in 1931 there was less land under wheat than at any time since the eighteenth century). And yet it was not the same. The horrors of 1914–18 had wrought a profound psychological change in the nation – a change easier to state than to define. In 1914 the framework of rural society, though under enormous pressures, was an ancient and apparently indestructible framework. It was a hierarchy of paternalism and mutual interdependence – labourers worked for tenant farmers who owed allegiance to large landlords. The squire (not forgetting his good lady) and the parson felt a joint responsibility for their people, especially for the poor and needy. Estates dwindled and changed hands; in some areas the traditional pattern had already been irretrievably broken. But the fundamental belief remained that this was the right order of things. It was a belief which imprisoned the out-of-work labourer in his native village and impelled the farmer to keep on workers he could not really afford to employ.

In 1918 the heirs of many great estates failed to return from Flanders as did most of the next generation of farmers and labourers. During the years of the Depression many wealthy families cut down on the numbers of their staff. They sold off farms to sitting tenants or to newcomers. They were financially crippled by death duties and found their large houses difficult or impossible to maintain. Halls, manor houses and mansions which had stood for centuries were transformed into grandiose granaries, were allowed to decay, were sold for institutional purposes or were demolished. Suffolk's lost heritage in these years includes the Jacobean magnificence of Easton Park, the Classical Revival splendours of Oakley Park and the Georgian stateliness of Livermere Hall. And there were many others.

In farming the tendency was now to work smaller units which could be managed with as few men as possible. Here mechanization was a distinct advantage. The tractor took over all the jobs which teams of horses and men had done before. Hiring equipment or combining with neighbours to buy it was cheaper in the long run than paying wages, especially after 1924 when the Agricultural Wages Act set up a county board to fix minimum wages. Moreover, the era of unbridled free trade had gone forever. From 1924 onwards state intervention increased; subsidies, rates relief, import tariffs and guaranteed prices all helped the farmer to eke a living from the soil. If he had sufficient capital he could avail himself of the many technical innovations coming from the laboratories and workshops of the land. But the most important new development of all was not the product of human ingenuity. During the war, farmers had been encouraged to grow sugar beet in order to reduce the country's dependence on imported cane sugar. This had been so successful that in 1924 the government offered a subsidy to beet producers. The crop was ideally suited to the heavy soil of central Suffolk and without delay a number of farmers combined to persuade a Hungarian company to build a sugar factory in Bury St Edmunds. 5,000 acres were immediately planted with beet and the acreage grew steadily.

It was during this period that one of the more characteristic features of the Suffolk landscape was banished by the decree of progress. In the mid-nineteenth century it was virtually impossible to stand anywhere in Suffolk without seeing a windmill. William Cobbett, visiting Ipswich in 1830, counted 17, all visible from the same spot, 'they are all painted and washed white; the sails are black; it was a fine morning, the wind was brisk, and their twirling all together added greatly to the beauty of the scene'. In 1926 there were 48 working mills left and by the outbreak of World War II this number had dwindled to 14. They had, of course, succumbed to the new sources of energy which rendered the wind obsolete. Steam and, later, diesel driven mills were set up in every town. They could handle large quantities of grain and, because of the new forms of transport, could serve a wide area. So, yet another cornerstone of village life was removed.

More fundamental still was the accelerating drift to the towns. For urban growth was as rapid as rural depopulation. Manufacturing and service industries were springing up and demanding labour. Councils and private speculators rushed to build dwellings to house the newcomers. Ipswich grew more rapidly than most and a correspondent on the *Gazette* was, in 1925, moved to complain:

Rope Walk . . . can hardly be described as a sylvan glade today. Bricks and mortar made into workmen's dwellings which are not fit for workmen to dwell in have altered it. But in old times there was a double row of trees the whole length of the Rope Walk, and under these the ships' ropes were spun out for use at the old shipyards when ships were built in Ipswich and had fair renown wherever they went. These were the days when Ipswich was sylvan Ipswich . . . I mourn the loss of The Grove, where Mrs Cobbold used to entertain His Majesty's Judges, all the beautiful trees felled, and blank space only left where one of the best bits of sylvan Ipswich used to be. Bricks and mortar are the rule today with rapacious landlords, who allot so many inches of land to 'eligible suburban villas', and where in the old days houses had their half-acre of garden planted with fruit trees; you now get about room to grow a poor fern or two, which quickly die of inanition . . . And so I might go on through the purlieus of St Matthew's parish, with Black Horse Lane and the old pub. of that name stood by itself in its own grounds . . . Now the space is built over as far as Broom Hill, and the inhabitants of the West end are clamouring for this spot to be preserved to them as another public park for the town.

But before we consider the growth of our towns in this period let us take a last look at village life, for the changes that occurred there constitute one of the most fundamental developments in the history of the last 500 years. The parish of Brandeston near Framlingham was typical enough. In 1842 it was a self-contained community of 555 souls. It had a fourteenth-century church with Perpendicular additions and a Tudor hall recently bought by Charles Austin Q.C., High Steward of Ipswich, J.P., Chairman of the Quarter Sessions, etc., etc. There was an ancient inn, though the 'Queen's Head' on its sign was Victoria's, and a new Congregational chapel. Henry Collins' mill stood on the edge of the village and is reputed to have had eight sails. Blacksmith, wheelwright, joiner, butcher, grocer, tailor, builder – whatever service the villagers required was available from among their own number, as a visitor observed about 1854:

> The blacksmith is ready at anyone's call
> To mend a horse shoe or a clock at the Hall,
> And his friend Mr. White, when he goes to the Hall
> If he wants him to go he will give him a call,
> Here's a wheeler, a butcher, and a man at his post
> And a Post master of all trades, quite a whole host,
> And a doctor of physic, who often times vows
> He can cure restive horses and raise fallen cows,
> The man at the Queen is a cute little chap
> He can make a cart well and stick to the tap,
> His porter is as fresh as the dew in the morn,
> And he serves it in metal instead of old horn,
> His gin, rum, and brandy are all very fine,
> His ale is first rate, and quite the crack is his wine,
> Then there's Bedwell the builder, upon a broad plan
> Ancient, modern, or commercial to suit any man,
> Emeny the mason is good at the wall
> With sound bricks and mortar it cannot well fall,
> A dealer who lives in one of those stages
> Recommends dairying with three useful ages,
> There's Brown for spring flowers, and a Garrod for collars,
> And Leeds the schoolmaster is one that next follows,
> The miller is clever and a good bargain strikes,
> He's a grocer and draper, and well in for Dykes,
> He's a farmer likewise, but is short of a barn,
> And he lives very near to the merchant named Stearn . . .

There were 13 farmers, and the rest of the working community were employed directly or indirectly in agriculture. On the rare occasions when a man needed to leave the village he would walk or go with the carter to Wickham Market where he could pick up the Royal Mail or the Lord Nelson coach to London.

A hundred years later the population of Brandeston was 312. The third and last generation of the Austins had left the Hall, which was on the point of becoming a boys' school. The Congregational chapel was closed. There was no trace of the windmill and the mill house was now the post office. There were eight farms employing between them some 20 or 30 men. The old stables of the Hall had been converted into flats. Hill House, a substantial Georgian residence, was a saddler's workshop. The forge was still operating but the nearby wheelwright had long since closed his shop. Some of the houses were empty and many, especially the thatched cottages, were in need of repair. The railway at nearby Hacheston Halt and Parham linked Brandeston with Ipswich and the world, and the Eastern Counties bus came through regularly. Villagers frequently went on shopping expeditions to Framlingham, Wickham Market and the county capital. And who were the villagers? Retired farmworkers and servants from the Hall; newcomers in search of rural seclusion; men and women who travelled to the nearby towns for work. Compare the names of Brandestonians in 1842 and 1947 and you find only a few that are identical.

The improvements in transport during this period brought the people of Suffolk many new opportunities for business and pleasure. By 1880 the county was criss-crossed by an interlinking mesh of railway lines, and branches connected such outlying places as Southwold, Felixstowe and Aldeburgh to the system. Most lines were served by the Great Eastern locomotives in their livery of royal blue with red lettering and polished brass fittings, which operated out of the domed, metropolitan entrepôt of Liverpool Street. Despite all the hissing, clanking haste of those far off steam days and the company's jealous reputation for punctuality, entrusted to the bustling guards with their watches and whistles, there was a friendly leisureliness about train travel, as one frequent holidaymaker of those years recalls:

We would sometimes be lucky with connections and manage to get a fast train as far as Saxmundham, but usually it would be the slow passenger and goods, stopping at every station. We would then choose a carriage as near as possible to the guard's van so that we could while away the long wait at each halt, watching the comings and goings . . . There would always be milk churns; and what a clattering and banging they made as the empty ones were manhandled along the platform with a kind of rolling motion, and the full ones dumped aboard from a metal tip-up trolley just big enough to take one churn. Then there were the sacks of mail, and the livestock, cackling, clucking, or cooing and poking their indignant heads through the openwork sides of their temporary wicker homes. Perhaps there would be a bicycle or two, some small farming implements, and lastly the trunks and dressbaskets, suitcases and grips, and all the usual paraphernalia of the travelling public. When all was aboard, the engine driver would alight from his cab, and with the guard and porter-cum-station master have a conflab . . . until it seemed the train would take root. But at last, with a 'See yer temorra bor!' the party would break up, the driver would climb aboard, the guard wave his flag, and we would chug-chug out of the station, only to repeat the same performance a mile or so further along the line. Eventually disembarking at Saxmundham, it was not unusual to find that the branch train to Leiston and Aldeburgh had cantankerously departed less than five minutes before . . . But a wait for the 'Winkle Express' was always well worthwhile.

In 1923 the many private railway concerns were compulsorily amalgamated into four large companies and the G.E.R. lost its identity within the London and North Eastern Railway (or, as it was caustically dubbed 'the Late and Never Early Railway').

In the sphere of road transport there was an almost bewildering amount of experimentation. Steam, electricity, diesel engines, petrol engines – all were tried and applied to a variety of machines – lorries, buses, trams, cars, motor-cycles. In the days before specialization any competent, small engineering firm could turn out a motor car, and many did. Brookes of Lowestoft operated between 1900 and 1913 before deciding to specialize in marine engines. Lindsays and Thorofare Motors of Woodbridge are names still mentioned in veteran car circles.

But the Suffolk giants such as Turners, Garretts and Ransome, Sims and Jefferies were also active in road transport.

At £400 and £500 each the custom built cars of those days were certainly for the rich only. It was not until after the 1914–18 war that omnibuses began to serve a wide area. The Eastern Counties Road Car Company began operating out of Ipswich in 1919 with four 'Tillings' 36-seated, double-decker buses. They had plenty of opposition: the Swiftsure, the Shamrock, Beeston's and the Blue Bird were just some of the small companies whose vehicles literally roamed the lanes plying for hire. There were no established routes or bus stops. Indeed timetables could be positively detrimental to trade. If a competitor knew that a certain bus was going to follow a certain route starting at a specific time he would send his own vehicle out a few minutes earlier to 'poach' all the customers. This free-for-all ceased in 1930 with the passing of the Road Traffic Act. Soon afterwards Eastern Counties bought out most of its rivals and established a virtual monopoly throughout East Anglia.

This was a period of continuing expansion for the east coast ports and resorts. Colonel George Tomlin of Nacton was the man behind the growth of Felixstowe. He owned about 25,000 acres in and around the little seaside village which enjoyed a modest poularity as a genteel holiday resort. He brought the railway there in 1877 and four years later he began the building of a dock at the mouth of the Orwell. It was opened in 1886 and Felixstowe was well set on the path to prosperity. The Great Eastern began regular boat services to the continent from Felixstowe and Harwich. Hotels were built, the largest being the Felix, which was eventually taken over by the railway. High-class summer villas and less exalted boarding houses emerged, and every summer the buses, trains and Rolls Royces trundled into the town bearing visitors bent on taking their pleasure in salubrious Felixstowe. The fisheries also flourished and it was not unusual for six truckloads of sprats to be carried off to London on the afternoon goods train.

Felixstowe flared – very literally – into the national news one day in April 1914. During the previous night the resort's

153

most exclusive hotel, the Bath Hotel, had been totally gutted by fire. Arson was immediately suspected, particularly when leaflets were picked up which had been scattered round the building: 'There can be no peace until women get the vote' and 'No vote means war'. A few days later two visitors to the town, Hilda Burkett (31) and Florence Tunks (26), were arrested and charged with the crime. During their various judicial hearings the two women behaved in the hysterical manner which we have now come to expect from fanatics whose devotion to a cause leads them into acts of terrorism. They shouted, laughed and ridiculed the court. 'I am not going to keep quiet,' cried Miss Burkett, when ordered to be silent, 'I have come here to enjoy myself'. Truculent and abusive to the last, they eventually left the assize court at Bury, screaming and shouting, to begin long spells of imprisonment and hard labour.

To return to the fishing industry, this period saw an incredible boom in herring production. Every day the 'fish special' left Lowestoft bound for London. These were the great days of the steam drifters, sturdy, long-range boats which made possible a far more systematic exploitation of the herring shoals. At the peak of the industry, in 1913, 1,760 drifters were operating out of Lowestoft and Yarmouth. In the Spring and Summer they fished the ground off Ireland and western Scotland, landing their catches at ports between Milford Haven and Stornaway. Working their way down the eastern coast, they engaged in 'home fishing' from September to the end of the year. Some of the catches were phenomenal (In 1913 ninety million fish were landed at Lowestoft and Yarmouth) and Lowestoft was very glad of the expert Scottish girls who followed the fishing fleets round the coast and whose deft fingers gutted the fish in very quick time. From Lowestoft (and what was true of Lowestoft was true to a lesser extent of Southwold) the herrings were exported direct to the continent or conveyed inland by train. After 1918 the general economic depression, the loss of men in the war and the depletion of the herring stocks all had their effect and by 1939 the number of operational drifters had been halved. Fishing was, however, still a thriving industry.

We cannot leave the coast without mentioning the selfless, sacrificial work of generations of lifeboatmen. The notorious storms of the North Sea which have for millenia battered our coast have taken the lives of countless fishermen and mariners. But always there have been men of the sea who have risked their own lives and boats to go to the aid of ships in distress. The lifeboat service, therefore, has no known beginning. However, it had its formal inauguration in Suffolk in 1800 when a group of gentlemen from the north-east of the county formed a Lifeboat Society and raised a subscription to provide a boat at Lowestoft. Throughout the century lifeboats were also established at Southwold, Dunwich, Aldeburgh and Bawdsey, though they were not all in operation at the same time. The stories of bravery well beyond the call of duty, of heroic rescues carried out almost nonchalantly as 'part of the job' are so many that choice becomes quite invidious. Some men became legends in their own lifetimes – Bob Hook and Jack Swan of Lowestoft, Ben Harrington of Southwold, James Cable and Joshua Chard of Aldeburgh.

Bob Hook's most famous exploit was his almost single-handed rescue of the brig *William* which went aground on Holm Sands in 1880. The tide had ebbed so far by the time Hook's crew reached the wreck that the boat could not approach. Without hesitation, Coxswain Hook tied a line around himself and, half swimming, half wading, made his way to the stranded *William* through cruelly pounding seas. Hook was a giant of a man but even so his survival, and the subsequent rescue of the *William's* crew was regarded as little short of a miracle. Jack Swan, Coxswain of the *Agnes Cross*, won an OBE in 1922 for bringing his boat in close to the wrecked *Hoplyn* during a furious E.N.E. autumn gale and bringing off the entire crew. One could fill a book with the exploits of the lifeboatmen. If every one of them who deserved a medal received one there would scarcely be metal enough to strike them.

These were not the only acts of bravery Suffolk men and women were called upon to perform. In the middle of the period covered in this chapter there occurred the appalling cataclysm of 'the war to end all wars'. The Suffolk coast was one of the first areas in Britain to experience an air raid. On the night of 15 April 1915 three German airships set off on what was to have been a raid on the industrial and dockland area of the Humber. In the darkness they lost their way and L5 dropped its load of six high explosive and 40 incendiary bombs on Lowestoft and Southwold. The most serious damage was done to a Lowestoft timber yard which was largely destroyed by fire.

As in other parts of the country women stepped into many of the jobs vacated by men – in the engineering workshops, in the offices and on the land. Many of them employed their feminine talents for care and concern in the medical services, which were strained to capacity during the war. At one hospital alone, the East Suffolk and Ipswich, 7,777 casualties were treated. New wards had to be added, and Broadwater, a large house in Belstead Road, was converted into an annexe. As well as this a hospital requisites depôt was opened in Northgate Street which sent over 2,000,000 bandages, dressings and medical supplies of every kind to hospitals at home and in the battle zones. Most people who could not or would not fight contributed in some way, giving time, money and energy to the war effort.

And the others – those who answered the call of Kitchener and the war cabinet? In 1914 and 1915 thousands of young Suffolk men volunteered for military service. Ipswich alone sent 10,000 to the war. The Suffolk Regiment was made up to a strength of 27 battalions. It saw action in all the major theatres of war – the Western Front, Gallipoli, Macedonia and Palestine. Appalling losses were suffered on the Somme and the Gallipoli beaches. The Regiment returned at last with two Victoria Crosses and minus 7,000 men.

It is worthwhile to pause at this point to consider just what the war meant to those who bore the brunt of it, not because it was any worse for Suffolk men than for others, but because it changed the attitudes of a generation and ensured that life 'back home' would never be the same again. In Ronald Blythe's *Akenfield* an old farm worker recalled why he joined the army and what happened to him:

I returned to my old farm at Akenfield for 11*s*. a week, but I was unsettled. When the farmer stopped my pay because it was raining and we couldn't thrash, I said to my seventeen-year-old mate, 'Bugger him. We'll go off and join the army . . .'

In my four month's training with the regiment I put on nearly a stone in weight and got a bit taller. They said it was the food but it was really because for the first time in my life there had been no strenuous work . . . village people in Suffolk in my day were worked to death. It literally happened. It is not a figure of speech. I was worked mercilessly . . .

He was sent to the Dardanelles and arrived at a place close to the front line.

That evening we wandered about on the dead ground and asked about friends of ours who had arrived a month or so ago. 'How is Ernie Taylor?' 'Ernie? – he's gone.' 'Have you seen Albert Paternoster?' 'Albert? – he's gone.' We learned that if 300 had gone but 700 were left, then this wasn't too bad. We then knew how unimportant our names were . . .

He survived Gallipoli, the Somme and a prisoner-of-war camp and was eventually demobbed.

The soldiers who got back to the village recovered very quickly. People who had lost their sons felt strange. Generally speaking, we were thankful that it was all over and we could get back to our work. Yet things *had* changed and people were different. The farm-workers who had been soldiers were looked at in a new way. There were a few more privileges around than there used to be. They'd let you take a rabbit or two, for instance. Before 1914, if you'd caught a rabbit, my God, the world would have come to an end! The sack was the least you'd get. We felt that there must be no slipping back to bad old ways and about 1920 we formed a branch of the Agricultural Labourers' Union.

Those last sentences sum up admirably the situation after the war – the delayed shock, the frenzied determination to get back to normal, the slow realization that things would never be the same again. Every parish raised its monument to the fallen and vowed never to forget. In honour of the pledge new hospital wings, playing fields, sports pavilions and other memorials were opened. Victory was celebrated with fêtes, dances and socials. The returning heroes were welcomed with joy and gratitude. But the gratitude did not extend to ensuring employment or improving working conditions. Men wandered from farm to farm, village to village looking for work. They joined unions if they could afford the dues but they had no bargaining strength; the jobs simply were not there. The problem of rural depression was an old one but the post war generation was not prepared to tackle it in an old way. The war had loosened society, broadened horizons, changed social attitudes and political aspirations. In 1920 a Labour M.P. was returned for South Norfolk. Perhaps it was the women who blazed the trail. Their achievement of the vote had shown that persistence, sacrifice, unity and violence could successfully challenge the establishment. Now the men voted with their feet. They severed their roots with the land. They moved to the towns and created what had scarcely existed in Suffolk before as a self-conscious unit – an urban working class.

During this period two important administrative changes occurred. In 1888 the county was divided into two regions, East Suffolk and West Suffolk. In 1913, after a thousand years, Suffolk once more had its own diocese: the huge diocese of Norwich was split in two and a new see created with its centre at Bury St Edmunds. There was some feeling at the time that this arrangement unduly favoured West Suffolk, so the bishop's residence and the administrative centre of the new diocese was located in Ipswich in order to balance the choice of St James', Bury, as the new Cathedral.

9. THROUGH THE LOOKING GLASS

The future is an unknown world, like a Looking-glass Land. Though not the same as the past, many points of reference connect them, and before we step through into it we do well to take a good, long look into the mirror we call history. For this mirror shows us ourselves in relationship to what has gone before. The distant past we can only see with difficulty, like the shadows of furniture in dark corners. The events of recent years stand out in clearer detail; we recognize them instantly; we have ideas and feelings about them. They are important to us because they have touched our own lives and not just the lives of unknown ancestors. But we should not be misled by this into thinking that for this reason recent history is more important in the grand scheme of things.

The war of 1939–45 involved Suffolk much more directly than its predecessor. Suffolk fishermen were at Dunkirk to help bring off the survivors of the first disastrous round of the conflict. Among those survivors were members of the 1st Battalion of the Suffolk Regiment who had lost hundreds of men in the winter of 1939–40, including their commanding officer. Even before the war began the county had given a lead in military preparedness to the rest of the nation. Dithering between reliance on conscription or a volunteer army, the politicians decided to launch a Territorial Army recruitment drive. In two months the Suffolk Regiment raised 2,060 men – an incredible record. The Twelfth went on to fight in many of the main – and some of the worst – theatres of war – Burma, North Africa, Singapore – and the 1st Battalion went back into Europe on 'D' Day.

Yet it was the war in the air which most closely involved Suffolk. Despite the renewed demand for increased agricultural output, thousands of productive acres were buried under concrete and tarmac to provide Britain with much needed airfields. Fighter squadrons based at such stations as Martlesham were involved in the Battle of Britain. Though the airfields south of the Thames were the ones most heavily committed in that conflict, it was No 11 Group Fighter Command whose headquarters were at Hornchurch, Essex, which was specifically charged with the defence of London, and many dog fights were seen in the clear skies over East Anglia during the beautiful summer of 1940. The most devastating raid carried out over Suffolk was on 15 August when a hundred German bombers pounded Martlesham. But the county soon had its revenge: the first bombing raids of German territory set out from Wattisham and Mildenhall in December and attacked industrial installations at Kiel, Bremmer and Mannheim.

Suffolk bases provided the hard core of Bomber Command. The headquarters of No 3 Group were at Mildenhall. From here many of the raids were organized which, for many months, proved to be the only effective offensive attacks on military and industrial targets and naval support missions aimed at enemy ports and harbours filled the period before March 1943 when the Allied air offensive began. The U.S. 8th Air Force had begun to arrive in 1942, bringing their 'Flying Fortresses', Douglases and Liberators to augment British Wellingtons, Halifaxes and Lancasters. More land and more buildings were requisitioned for airfields and operations centres. Nissen huts and hangars studded the landscape. Thousands upon thousands of bombers and fighter support craft stood like strange new crops amid the wheat and beet fields. Suffolk people stood in their streets, lanes and gardens to watch the droning procession of outward going planes bent on the destruction of the enemy. Just as familiar were the squadrons – always smaller – which returned, and the damaged singletons coughing their low-level way over the treetops, desperately trying to regain their bases – and sometimes failing.

If Britain owes her survival in 1940 to 'the Few' she also owes it to the back-room boys who perfected radar. Chief among them was Robert Watson-Watt who carried out his researches at Orfordness in the mid-1930s. In 1936 he moved his equipment to Bawdsey Manor and it was there the prototype of chain home radar stations was established. Many of these lined the east and south coasts by the time war broke out. They proved a more successful means of defence than the bunkers and the concrete and barbed wire paraphernalia which strewed our beaches would ever have done if the Nazis had crossed the Channel. Not far away from Bawdsey one of the last dramatic events of the war was enacted. On 13 May 1945 Admiral Karl Bruening surrendered the Nazi E boat fleet to his opposite number at Felixstowe. As well as being the headquarters of the British motor torpedo-boat fleet, Felixstowe was the main base for the Short Sunderland flying boats which did such sterling work rescuing the crews of stricken ships and ditched aeroplanes.

The ending of World War II did not come as abruptly as that of the earlier conflict. Certainly Suffolk celebrated V.E. Day and V.J. Day, and welcomed her heroes back from the front and shared in the 'great betrayal' by returning Labour members in some of her constituencies, but most of the basic realities of life continued: our young men continued to be conscripted for two years' National Service; rationing was still with us and so were the Americans. We had a curious love-hate relationship with the Americans: we touched them for gum, cigarettes and nylons and resented them getting too interested in our women; we were amused at the way they rushed round our 'quaint' villages with their cameras and made enthusiastic brass rubbings in our churches but we were not amused when they told us how they had won 'our' war.

Then, gradually, the airfields were abandoned, the Nissen huts were sold off to farmers, and the Defence Ministry personnel went back to London, leaving to decay the country houses they had occupied. Suffolk slipped back into its old ways – underemployment, rural depopulation, low land and property values. Urban growth continued – for the most part unimaginatively – as council estates were built to replace war damage and cater for the growing town populations. Railway traffic declined and several branch lines, such as the Long Melford to Bury St Edmunds and sections of the Waveney Valley, had closed before the celebrated 'Beeching axe' was wielded in 1963. Suffolk did not share in the slow growth of national prosperity of the 1950s. Then, suddenly, came the boom. Within a decade Suffolk became England's fastest growing county.

It began in the early 1960s and its manifestations were many. New industries came to the town. Issues of planned town growth now became urgent. Old properties – particularly thatched cottages and timber-framed farmhouses – were eagerly sought. Increasing trade crammed the county's main roads with lorries and forced an expansion and improvement of port facilities. Agriculture was revitalized: farmers bought new equipment and cultivated their land far more intensively than ever before. The population of the county increased by over 18 per cent (the national average was 5.8 per cent) in the decade 1961–71.

There were many reasons for this unprecedented growth, which brough Suffolk a prosperity it had not known since the great days of the cloth trade. Paradoxically, Suffolk's very depression gave a boost to new development. Most of the county was within 80 miles of London and served by reasonable road and rail connections. Some of its ports were no further from the capital than those of Kent and they were a great deal closer to the industrial Midlands and North. Some of Suffolk's most beautiful countryside was no further from the metropolis than the 'stockbroker belt' of Sussex, Hampshire, Wiltshire, Berkshire and Buckinghamshire. Yet land and property prices in Suffolk were less than half of what they were in the desirable areas of these other counties. Population was now more mobile, and light industry less tied to traditional centres. Thus, neglected Suffolk was ready to be rediscovered. Companies escaping from high overheads realized that they could find the facilities and labour they required in Ipswich, Bury, Sudbury and Haverhill. Executives discovered that they could live in an area of great peace and beauty and yet be within commuting distance of their City desks. Moreover, the shift in the balance of international trade focused attention once more on the eastern approaches. When the bulk of Britain's trade was with the Empire and America it was logical that London, Southhampton and Liverpool should have been our main ports. Our railway network was constructed in such a way as to convey manufactured goods to these ports. But the Empire was disbanded and Britain was drawn, inevitably but at times unwillingly, into the European Common Market. More and more industrial traffic took to the road; heavy lorries at first, then containers. Now producers were looking for the shortest routes to the continent. Many of them lay through Suffolk. More and more British people and foreign visitors discovered the attractions of Suffolk. They realized that a century or more of economic stagnation had preserved from thoughtless development one of the loveliest corners of England. They came in increasing numbers in their, now ubiquitous, motor cars to spend quiet family holidays at the coast, to tour the unspoilt villages, to admire the half-timbering, the thatch, the pargetting and the great wool churches. Some decided to stake a claim by buying up old cottages for 'week-ending' or retirement.

These events have brought changes to the county which can only be called revolutionary, yet they are still too recent to invite accurate assessment; we can only catalogue some of the more important. The most astonishing development is that the population, which had been decreasing for over a century, jumped from 475,000 in 1951 to 560,000 in 1961. Most of this increase was in West Suffolk (a similar population growth had occurred in the Ipswich area during the late 'fifties and had then levelled out). The growth of Bury, Haverhill and Sudbury

accounts largely for the extra population. These were designated in the mid-1950s as London overspill areas. Carefully
planned industrial and housing estates were built and a variety
of service industries and light engineering concerns moved
their machines and desks to spacious premises from whose
windows the workers could actually see trees and green fields.
In 1973 the Bury St Edmunds sugar beet factory was considerably enlarged by the building of two huge new silos. It is
now the largest plant of its kind in Europe and is playing an
important part in bringing Britain closer to the goal of self-
sufficiency in this product.

However, development was not restricted to the western side
of the county. The growth of Ipswich has largely been as a
result of migration from *within* Suffolk. Even so its population
increased from 100,000 to 122,000 between the end of the war
and 1971. It is the only urban centre in the county to have suffered the fate of many large towns and cities – haphazard and
largely unplanned development over many years. Farmers can
still remember when Ipswich was just a large market town,
where they could hail one another across the street. Now dual
carriageways and one-way systems attempt to relieve its con-
gested centre, while old and new buildings jostle each other in
irredeemable incongruity.

A lonely stretch of coast near Leiston was the site of another
important development. Here, at Sizewell, Britain's second
nuclear power station was built in the early 1960s. In 1966
power began surging out from the grey, cuboid plant into the
national grid. Now Sizewell's 580,000 kilowatts go a long way
towards meeting eastern England's electricity needs.

But the most remarkable success story of all is that of Felixstowe docks. In 1955 the Felixstowe Dock and Railway Company had on its hands a dilapidated dock which needed dredging,
and warehouses, quays and sea walls showing signs of severe
storm damage. The total labour force was nine men. Today the
dock area covers hundreds of acres (many of them reclaimed) of
spacious wharves, warehouses and storage areas equipped with
the latest cargo handling machinery. The transformation

began in 1956 and was the direct result of foresight and careful planning. Calculating that changing trade patterns and Felixstowe's proximity to Rotterdam and Antwerp provided exciting prospects for an efficient, well-equipped port, the Company's directors launched a £3 million project to create a new deep water berth geared to the latest bulk transportation technique – containerization. That accomplished, another £8 million were set aside for an oil jetty and bulk liquid storage facilities. Just to show that Felixstowe can handle every kind of traffic, a passenger terminal was opened in 1975. Felixstowe dock has acquired a reputation for fast, efficient handling of all types of cargo. Consignments to and from the port can easily reach the major industrial centres by road or rail. The only question mark standing against Felixstowe dock's continued success is whether it can survive the planned nationalization scheme.

The development of new industry and the growth of the east coast ports have necessitated a considerable programme of trunk road improvement. By the mid-1970s work was well in hand and at a time when economic stringency was forcing the curtailment of other roadbuilding schemes, East Anglia's new roads were being given priority treatment. Most of the A12, the London–Ipswich road, had been made into dual carriageway. The A45, the artery linking Ipswich and Felixstowe with the Midlands and the north-south motorways, had been considerably improved. Stowmarket, Bury St Edmunds and, that most notorious of all bottlenecks, Newmarket had been by-passed. By the end of the decade this road should have fast dual carriageway for most of its length. By then, also, the new A11/M11, London–Norwich, road will be nearing completion. When that happens, Suffolk's isolation really will be a thing of the past.

Farming, although it now employs fewer people than ever before, is still Suffolk's largest single industry. Accessibility to internal and European markets has led to a certain amount of diversity. There are numerous farmers specializing in poultry, pigs and dairying. Yet persistently high world grain prices have led to intensive production of what the heavy soils of central Suffolk are best suited for – cereals. The tendency for large estates to be split up and fields to remain unploughed has been dramatically reversed. Nowadays the larger the unit, the more economical the farm. Every producer is determined to get the maximum yield from his acres. To this end, hedges, copses and ditches have disappeared; poor land has been made fertile with chemical fertilizers; fields have been made as large as possible so that the tractor and the combine harvester can work them with greater ease. Today's Suffolk farmer is a hard professional – he has to be. The profits of his labour must be taken while they are there, for he remembers the old days, and who knows what is round the corner?

Suffolk has found it difficult to come to terms with tourism. Having been ignored by outsiders for so long, she was in no hurry to 'dress up for visitors'. Even the established holiday resorts – Aldeburgh, Southwold, Dunwich, Felixstowe – are genteel places; they do not bristle with amusement arcades, Wimpy bars and the assorted paraphernalia that urban man seems to expect at the seaside. Hedgerows and windows do not bristle with offers of 'Teas' and 'Accomodation'. Suffolk is more like a coy maiden prepared to be discovered than an accomplished seductress thrusting her charms at every eligible passer-by. Yet year by year more people do discover her charms, and a surprising number of visitors have staked out their own claims. They have bought and 'done up' labourers' cottages and farm buildings. So great was the demand for even derelict old properties that prices trebled in the period 1969–1973. The village community in Suffolk had already been loosened so the arrival of these strangers cannot be said to have disrupted a traditional culture. Only in those areas where the newcomers congregated in large numbers was real cultural damage inflicted.

Suffolk has remained a haven for artists, writers and musicians. Indeed, if the county had any need to justify its existence it would be sufficient to read the roll call of those who have found their spiritual home within its borders: Alfred Munnings, Angus Wilson, Peter Pears, William Alwyn, Hammond Innes, Reginald Brill, Ronald Blythe, Gilbert Spencer, Benjamin Britten. All of them have drawn inspiration from the land and people of Suffolk – just think of *Peter Grimes*.

Mention of Benjamin Britten brings us to Suffolk's great contribution to the artistic life of Britain – the Aldeburgh Festival. The composer returned from the U.S.A. in 1947 to live at Aldeburgh and almost at once conceived the idea of holding a festival of arts. It began in a small way in the following year and like Topsy, it 'just growed'. The activities – concerts, recitals, operas, exhibitions – multiplied and every suitable local building was used. Many great artists came to perform and the public came, from all over the world, to listen. Britten and his colleagues long felt the need for a large concert hall with good acoustics but they did not want to move the festival away from Aldeburgh and the cost of building a new hall was prohibitive. In October 1965 the lease of part of a disused maltings at Snape became available. It was a lovely spot overlooking the Alde and the festival organizers were soon busy with architects and builders. The concert hall that emerged preserved the character of the original building while providing an airy, yet intimate, atmosphere for making music. The Queen opened the building on 2 June 1967 and it immediately became one of England's best-loved concert halls.

Two years later disaster struck. On 7 June 1969 the Maltings was burned out. Only the smoke-blackened walls were left standing. Shock was swiftly followed by a determination that the concert hall must be rebuilt. Gifts poured in from music lovers the world over. In less than 42 weeks the hall had been reconstructed to the original design. Nor did the organizers rest there: money was soon being accumulated to extend the complex by adding rehearsal rooms, a music library, an art gallery, an exhibition hall and other facilities.

Suffolk too, has recovered from apparent disaster and now stands poised to face an exciting future. In 1974 the Department of the Environment produced a report called *Strategic Choice for East Anglia*. It forecast a population of over 800,000 in

Suffolk by the end of the century. It saw the major towns growing much larger and suggested that the county would inevitably lose some of its individuality.

> We know . . . that the change and the growth . . . will make
> East Anglia more like other places. For some, this will mean
> that growth should be resisted, and the opportunities which
> it brings should be foregone. Whether or not we sympathize
> with this point of view, we do not think it is practicable.
> Much of the change and growth that is coming cannot be
> prevented by any of the means that is likely to be available.
> The only realistic approach is to recognize this, and take
> firm, positive steps to maintain and even enhance the envi-
> ronment of the region, using the extra resources that growth
> will bring . . .

The people of Suffolk have already had to face up to many of the
problems brought about by current changes. For there are
areas in which the interests of farmers, businessmen, holidaymakers and country dwellers inevitably clash. When the
farmer burns down hedges, sprays insecticides indiscriminately and ploughs up footpaths he has the con-
servationists down on him like a ton of bricks. When schedule-
conscious truck drivers thunder their way through villages
there are angry protests. Every new building project is
examined avidly by environmentalists. Many local and coun-
trywide organizations have been formed to resist specific
threats to our heritage or to conserve places of beauty and historic interest in general. Societies like the Suffolk Preservation
Society and the Suffolk Historic Churches Trust do splendid
work. Sometimes they win; sometimes they give way to 'progress'; always they make people aware of the problem.

For Suffolk is now in a unique position. It has an incredibly
rich and well preserved heritage. It has a distinct county identity. It has kept all this intact until the recent decades of our
hectic century. Now, a bustling, energetic, industrial age is
forcing itself upon the county. It is a direct confrontation, and
Suffolk has the choice of what to make of it. In the past com-

mercialization has crept up on other areas unawares and the results have usually been disastrous. To a large extent Suffolk has the ability to choose its own destiny. Those of you who have followed my story this far and have observed the way this county has come through triumph and tragedy, prosperity and depression, will probably think, as I do, that the choice is in excellent hands.

BIBLIOGRAPHY

GENERAL

Victoria County History of Suffolk, 2 volumes, 1907, 1911
R. Rainbird Clarke: *East Anglia*, 1960
M. Bates: *East Anglia*, 1974

CHAPTER ONE

J. R. Moir: *The Antiquity of Man in East Anglia*, 1926
T. Holmes: *Ancient Britain and the Invasion of Julius Caesar*, 1917
L. Cottrell: *The Roman Forts of The Saxon Shore*, 1954
J. M. Scott: *Boadicea*, 1975

CHAPTER TWO

R. Rainbird Clarke: *East Anglia*, 1960
M. Gallyon: *The Early Church in Eastern England*, 1973
R. Bruce-Mitford: *The Sutton Hoo Ship Burial*, 1947
R. Bruce-Mitford: *The Sutton Hoo Ship Burial*, 1972
R. Bruce-Mitford: *Aspects of Anglo-Saxon Archaeology: Sutton Hoo and other discoveries*, 1975
M. Bates: *East Anglia*, 1974
A. Goodwin: *The Abbey of St Edmundsbury*, 1931

CHAPTER THREE

H. Munro Cautley: *Suffolk Churches and Their Treasures* (1937)

A. Goodwin: *The Abbey of St Edmundsbury* (1931)
Nigel Heard: *Wool: East Anglia's Golden Fleece* (1970)
Bury St Edmunds Official Guide (1970)

CHAPTER FOUR
A. Simpson: *The Wealth of the Gentry 1540–1660* (1961)
M. Campbell: *The English Yeoman* (1960)
A. Hassell Smith: *County and Court, Government and Politics in Norfolk 1558–1603* (1974)
W. A. Copinger: *Manors of Suffolk* (7 volumes, 1905–1912)
B. McLenagh: *The Springs of Lavenham* (1924)
W. C. Metcalfe (ed): *The Visitations of Suffolk* (1882)

CHAPTER FIVE
R. C. Winthrop: *The Life and Letters of John Winthrop* (2 volumes 1864–7)
A. Everitt: *Suffolk in the Great Rebellion* (1960)
N. Heard: *Wool, East Anglia's Golden Fleece* (1970)

CHAPTER SIX
The Diary of John Evelyn
Daniel Defoe: *A Tour of the Whole of Great Britain* (1724–6)
Daniel Defoe: *A particular and Diverting Account of Whatever is Curious and Worth Observation* (1724)
Arthur Young: *A General View of the Agriculture of the County of Suffolk* (1794)

CHAPTER SEVEN
Arthur Young: *A General View of the Agriculture of the County of Suffolk* (1794)
Julian Tennyson: *Suffolk Scene* (1973)
Harold A. E. Day: *East Anglian Painters*, Vol I (1967)

CHAPTER EIGHT
J. Mitchley: *The Story of the Lowestoft Lifeboats* (1974)
R. Blythe: *Akenfield, Portrait of an English Village* (1972)
A Survey of the Parish of Brandeston (1971)

G. Moir: The Suffolk Regiment (1969)
H. Ryder Haggard: *A Farmer's Yearbook* (1899)

CHAPTER NINE
J. T. Appleby: *Suffolk Summer* (1948)
Strategic Choice for East Anglia HMSO (1974)

INDEX